Hong Kong Fantasies

Table of Contents

Why Fantasize?

This book fantasizes that Hong Kong – a city struggling to hold on to its reputation as a world financial centre, a global shopping Valhalla, and a liveable city with compelling architecture and magnificent nature – makes a comeback as an exemplary world-class city. What does it take, in our global economy, to be a world-class city? It's no longer enough to look at a city's GDP, its rate of tourism, its conference centres, stadiums, or shopping centres to evaluate its performance. Great cities have always offered a more fundamental, more abstract quality – a sense of well-being among citizens and visitors. This book attempts to define that quality, and to explore how the design of urban space can enhance it.

As our planet becomes increasingly urban, it is essential to set new standards for our cities, and to reassess the relationship between citizenship, well-being and the urban environment. Taking Hong Kong as a test case, Hong Kong Fantasies proposes a more expansive definition of 'world-class'. These new standards could help to raise the bar of urban life globally, and create cities that will be emulated not simply for their economic performance, but for the civic values they display and promote. This fictional urban resuscitation reveals not only the shortcomings of Hong Kong, but also the flaws in the tools with which we assess all cities. In order to improve our cities, we may also have to refine our standards of judgment.

The Degradation of World-Class

'The good city is a negotiation between form and life – the city's structure and its residents' activities.' [1]

Jan Gehl

'World-class', according to the Merriam-Webster Dictionary, means 'being of the highest calibre in the world'. The term is meant to identify the exceptional, to distinguish the extraordinary. Not just cities, but products, services and people – athletes, musicians, writers, etc. – can be described as world-class. Theoretically, to be in the world-class league is to serve as an ideal to the rest of the world – a benchmark.

In recent decades, institutions and companies have claimed this, and other elusive phrases, as shortcuts to success. In the 1980s, many global and regional firms, in pursuit of a competitive edge, began to strive for world-class status. For three decades now, these companies have been lavishing the global market with their mainstream products and standardized services. They have set up global guidelines, principles and standards, and use worldwide branding techniques to create their own 'lifestyles' and open new markets. [2] More recently, cities have followed this business trend; determined to achieve world-class distinction, many have embarked on self-improvement campaigns, marketing the qualities that will help them stand out in the global arena.

But these days, superlatives like 'world-class', 'world's greatest' and 'world's best' have a reduced impact; they have lost their meaning and exclusivity. Rather than representing an international standard of excellence, the term 'world-class' has become another empty, image-building adjective – a chameleonic marketing concept that seems to suit nearly everything and everyone that aspires to it. But despite its degradation, 'world-class' somehow continues to suggest a certain power, an intangible charisma that comes with implicit high standards and outstanding performance. What would it take to make this aura concrete – to give 'world-class' meaning for today's cities in the global economy? What if we look at the city as another product or service? If the common denominator of every quest for quality is customer satisfaction, who are the city's 'customers'? How can the city best serve them? What level of quality does it need to deliver?

The fundamental promise of city life is to offer community, civility, citizenship and a prosperous economic climate, as well as a foundation of common human values. These values include: the balance of rights and responsibilities; the civil liberty that enables citizens to address their physical, psychological and spiritual needs; a sense of community or social belonging; the everyday courtesies that make life safe, peaceful and pleasant; access to the day-to-day activities that people carry-out to achieve their goals – both personal and professional; and the opportunities for economic and social advancement that make life secure and fulfilling.

This sense of security and fulfilment starts with the physical environment of the city – an environment that is conducive to a sense of 'being, belonging and becoming'[3] among its citizens. To conform and measure up to this desire, cities need to preserve and improve upon what is already good, while creating opportunities to enable change and stimulate new lifestyles and markets. This study merges social and spatial values in cities, to arrive at new standards of judgement.

Greatness is Subjective

'We have to escape from the Ranking Rat Race. In the Global economy, what you need are many cities, not one'. [4]

Bill Hangley Jr.

In newspapers and magazines, on internet-forums and news programs across the media – wherever we turn, there's another version of 'the greatest city' debate. New York is still the best . . . or was it London . . . or maybe Paris again?

According to *the Quality of Living Index* by Mercer (2010), Vienna is number one, Zurich number two, and in third place – Geneva. The idea that many people would rather live in a city like Geneva than in Paris (34), New York (49), London (39), or Hong Kong (71), may seem peculiar. How could these modest cities achieve such high rankings? And why do American cities appear below the top 30, with Honolulu in 31st place? Why are only four Asian cities represented in the top 50, namely Singapore (28), Tokyo (40), and Kobe and Yokohama, which share 41st place with Barcelona and Milan? [5]

The top three cities may not host the richest companies, attract the most tourists, run the busiest airports, or provide citizens with the best-connected public transport. Instead, according to Mercer's survey, they offer a more abstract, qualitative achievement: the world's best living conditions. The problem with surveys that measure qualitative as well as quantitative aspects of city life is that the criteria for what constitutes 'quality of life' cannot be measured objectively – nor can it be standardized. Mercer analyses and measures living conditions by looking at 39 factors that are grouped into ten categories: (1) political and social environment (political stability, crime, law enforcement, etc); (2) economic environment (currency exchange regulations, banking services, etc); (3) socio-cultural environment (censorship, limitations on personal freedom, etc); (4) health and sanitation (medical supplies and services, infectious diseases, sewage, waste disposal, air pollution, etc); (5) schools and education (standard and availability of international schools, etc); (6) public services and transportation (electricity, water, public transport, traffic congestion, etc); (7) recreation (restaurants, theatres, cinemas, sports and leisure, etc); (8) consumer goods (availability of food/daily consumption items, cars, etc); (9) housing (housing, household appliances, furniture, maintenance services, etc); and (10) natural environment (climate, record of natural disasters). [6]

Although Mercer, one of the world's largest human resource consulting firms, claims that its survey is objective, the selection of factors and indicators, and the design of its questionnaires, are by definition subjective. In fact, Mercer's *Quality of Living Index* was established for expatriates; it provides qualitative as well as quantitative information about the cities where expatriates from anywhere in the world tend to work and live.

Other studies, like *the Global Cities Index*, *the Global Financial Cities Index* and *the Quality-of-Life Index* have tried, from different perspectives, to define what makes a city great, or exceptional. What do these indexes tell us? What values do they consider in measuring the city?

The Global Cities Index is a joint research project by *Foreign Policy Magazine*, the management consulting firm A. T. Kearney and the Chicago Council on Global Affairs. It aims to measure how much 'sway a city has over what happens beyond its own borders – its influence on and integration with global markets, culture, and innovation.' [7]

The Global Cities Index ranks cities of more than one million inhabitants according to 25 metrics applied to five areas: (1) business activity, (2) human capital, (3) information exchange, (4) cultural experience and (5) political engagement. The data ranges from the number of 'global company headquarters to the size of its capital markets and the flow of goods through its airports and ports, as well as factors such as the number of embassies, think tanks, political organizations, and museums.' [8] Taken as a whole, this joint study creates a platform that feeds the discussion on how cosmopolitan – or provincial – cities actually are. According to the initiators of this study, the most sophisticated and globally active city is New York City, followed by London (2) and Tokyo (3). [9]

The annually published *Global Financial Cities Index* (GFCI) by the Z/Yen Group, rates and ranks 'major financial centres of the world in terms of competitiveness.' Fourteen dimensions of competitiveness are measured and quantified according to over 57 instrumental factors based on the existing rankings of the most competitive global financial centres. These instrumental factors are grouped according to their relevance to: (1) people, (2) the business environment, (3) market access, (4) infrastructure and (5) general competitiveness.

The GFCI relies on both existing instrumental factors and self-constructed assessments by respondents. It responds to growth, new investment, and innovation in financial centres. Because the system is updated annually, it reflect[s] evolution in the long-term competitiveness of financial centres and] changes in financial centres globally.' [10]

This index, commissioned by the City of London, was first published in March 2007. Since then, no city has managed to beat out London as the number one city.

The Economist Intelligence Unit's (EIU) 'Quality-of-life Index' from *the Global Liveability Report 2010* uses over 30 qualitative and quantitative factors across five broad categories including: (1) stability, (2) healthcare, (3) culture and environment, (4) education and (5) infrastructure. [11]

Similar to *the Quality of Living Index* by Mercer, this index claims that it is meant for 'employers assigning hardship allowances as part of expatriate relocation packages' [12] According to the Economist Intelligence Unit, Vancouver was ranked as the most liveable global city in 2010. Other top liveable global cities are Vienna (2) and Melbourne (3). [13]

In addition to these economically-oriented analyses, there are other, more journalistic definitions that emphasize social qualities – like the 'most stylish' cities by Forbes (2009), and the 'most liveable cities' by Monocle (2010). Both Forbes and Monocle tend to evaluate cities according to their

status as cultural and trendy centres of the world.
Forbes ranks Paris as the world's number one 'most stylish city' followed by Milan (2) and New York (3). [14] Forbes's ranking represents cities that have made notable contributions to the field of design, and fashion in particular.

The list reflects the idea that fashion plays a leading role in any city's cultural evolution and identity. Forbes's ranking (2009) is based on the 2009 *Anholt-GfK Roper City Brands Index*, which represents the 'consumer perception of the image and reputation of 50 major cities worldwide'. It measures cities according to criteria like lifestyle, buzz, multiculturalism, cultural life and attractiveness. Respondents were asked to rank 50 cities on such varied subjects as climate, physical attractiveness, restaurants and nightlife.

Monocle's *Top 25 Most Liveable Cities* measures the cultural footprints of cities. It was created to identify cities that are home to happy and culturally inclined people. Monocle's evaluation looks beyond economics and politics and focuses on liveability factors such as restaurants, green space, response time for emergency services, local entertainment and the ease of starting businesses. In 2010, Monocle ranked Munich as the world's most liveable city with the best cultural footprint on the planet, followed by Copenhagen (2) and Zurich (3). [15]

Lonely Planet showcases what it calls 'best cities' in *The Cities Book: A Journey through the Best Cities in the World*, published in 2006.[16] 'Best', in this case, means the '200 most vibrant, diverse, hypnotic and chaotic cities in the world'. It seems almost a cliché that Paris is ranked as the best and most vibrant city on the planet followed by New York (2) and Sydney (3). The image of Paris as the city with the most chic and elegant lifestyle, food and fashion is burned into the global, popular culture. Paris – *la cité de la lumière* – could degenerate for many years without losing its reputation. However, Lonely Planet's list of the 200 most vibrant cities is ranked by people who, according to Lonely Planet, 'know their cities'. These cities are evaluated according to their overall strengths and weaknesses; export and import products; and cultural life and assets.

Another ranking, Askmen.com, a lifestyle portal for men (2009), lists 29

world cities according to their appeal to heterosexual men. In these 'hottest cities', with Chicago at the top, it is 'easy to meet women . . . professional opportunities abound, and . . . [men] can easily get outside, whether it be to a world-class stadium to watch a game or to the beach'. [17] Cities are judged on features like weather (based on the deviation from the average temperature in Askmen's ideal weather city – Los Angeles), cost-of-living (based on how the city scores on Mercer's cost-of-living index and Askmen's iPod and Nissan 370Z indices), professional life (based on the average income and the amount of guaranteed paid vacation), dating (based on the ratio of women to men and on how educated the city's women are), 'night on the town'
(based on the city's nightlife, culinary scene and new openings for 2010), 'day on the town' (based on the city's cultural calendar, availability of menswear and efficiency of public transit), and the 'fresh air factor' (based on the city's proximity to beaches and mountains, and the quality of its green spaces).

As varied as they may seem, these indexing concepts of 'best', 'most' or 'greatest' cities have one thing in common: all of their authors have tried to establish criteria by which to measure cities' economic performance and level of urban culture. The statistical concepts drawn by these authors may be correct, but the combination of objective economical factors with subjective social and cultural factors and interpretations can be inaccurate and misleading.

Much can be learned from such evaluations about the economic performance of a locality; but at the same time, the credibility of these ratings is dubious. They reduce the complexity of city life to a collection of abstract indices that cannot reflect the volatile and interdependent systems that compose our cities. Undoubtedly, by defining particular qualities as attractive, studies like these feed the competition amongst cities and inevitably encourage qualitative improvements. They generate new, not necessarily accurate rankings. But more importantly, not one of these indexes looks at cities as densely organized entities or takes all users of the city into account; none develop criteria by which the physical or built environment can be measured or judged. These indexing systems are not meant to guide responsible development that nurtures liveability of our cities. They lack focus on quantitative and qualitative aspects of spatial urban planning and architectural development. Despite the many systems of evaluation with scientific intentions, the concept of the 'great city' remains ambiguous.

Setting Higher Standards

The Need for City Data

'Yet the gross national product does not allow for the health of our children, the quality of their education, or the joy of their play. It does not include the beauty of our poetry or the strength of our marriages; the intelligence of our public debate or the integrity of our public officials. It measures neither our wit nor our courage; neither our wisdom nor our learning; neither our compassion nor our devotion to our country; it measures everything, in short, except that which makes life worthwhile'. [18]

Robert F. Kennedy

It is no longer enough for a city 'just' to be a global financial centre or a Valhalla for shopping addicts, to have a handful of iconic landmarks, to host a global event, or to boast a high Gross Domestic Product (GDP). [19] **As our planet becomes increasingly urban, and competition among cities intensifies, it is essential to set new urban quality standards that look beyond economic performance and values. Can a term like 'world-class' be applied more systematically, in order to establish a context, or framework, within which future cities can evolve? Can we introduce a tool to help formulate and standardize goals for our cities?**

A more expansive definition of 'world-class' could raise the bar for urban life and create cities that are emulated not simply for their economic performance, but also for the civic, urban and architectural values they display and promote.

In order to evaluate cities on these terms, a new kind of global instrument is needed: one that measures quality of life as a component of the built environment only; one that reflects the interdependence of the architectural and the social; one that measures performance, capacities and efficiencies within the collective dimensions of the built environment: density, diversity and connectivity. Such a tool would help cities adapt physically to world-class standards and to the needs of their citizens and users.

Despite an abundance of data on countries, comparable information on cities is scarce. Most comes from censuses; national surveys; global statistical organizations as for example the World Bank, World Health Organization or the United Nations; from consultancy firms; or from public or private companies. Cities need to produce data – some current, some historical – that reflects the psychological and physical well-being of its 'customers' ¬– families, children, singles, elderly, disabled people, tourists, artists, business people, etc. This data would make it possible to evaluate cities' environmental, spatial, socio-cultural and socio-economic conditions. It would provide the specific information needed to upgrade urban fabric, urban performance, and ultimately the well-being of urban populations.
At present, there exists no major indicator that relates well-being concerns to important physical environmental issues as density, diversity and connectivity.

What Makes a World-Class City?

[A World Class City is] 'a major international destination. Most often it's a major international political, cultural or commercial center. [It] includes cities of all sizes and not just the world's largest. A world class city is an exciting place to visit and has plenty of culture' [20]

www.urbandictionary.com

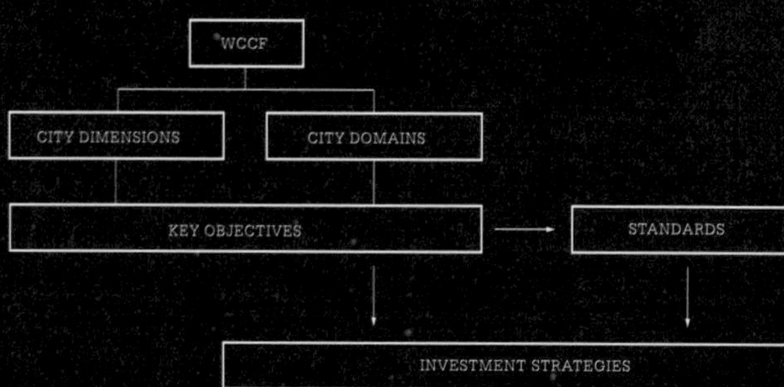

The World Class City Framework (WCCF) [fig. 1]

How can cities develop toward a world-class condition? The Why Factory's World-Class City Framework (WCCF) [fig. 1] **aims to establish a direction and provoke a public debate on the creation of a world-class city league. This framework defines a new set of spatial standards for world-class cities; these standards embrace high density, diversity and connectivity in order to promote a socially and environmentally engaged society. The WCCF also assembles indicators that make it possible to observe and measure the spatial and socio-economic performance of a city, and the satisfaction of its customers.**

Three basic dimensions are central to world-class city development: density, diversity and connectivity. These three dimensions form a framework upon which the spatial and socio-economic values of the world-class city can be developed. [fig. 2] Together, they embody architectural as well as social responsibilities to sustain the key attributes of human habitation – safety, health, mobility, aesthetics, recreation and leisure, economic opportunity and personal freedom.

While popular city indexing systems measure economic performance of cities, the WCCF is a tool to help develop a dense, diversified and hyper-connected city space. From this perspective, architecture emerges as an important socio-spatial agent – an interactive scripting device with the ability to create physical and emotional experiences; a tool that can improve, direct and nurture the functionality and evolution of world-class city life and the well-being of citizens and users.

Density, Diversity and Connectivity

'A city is the characteristic physical and social unit of civilization. It possesses size, density, grain, outline and pattern. The people who live in it shape these properties and are shaped by them.' [21]

Kevin Lynch

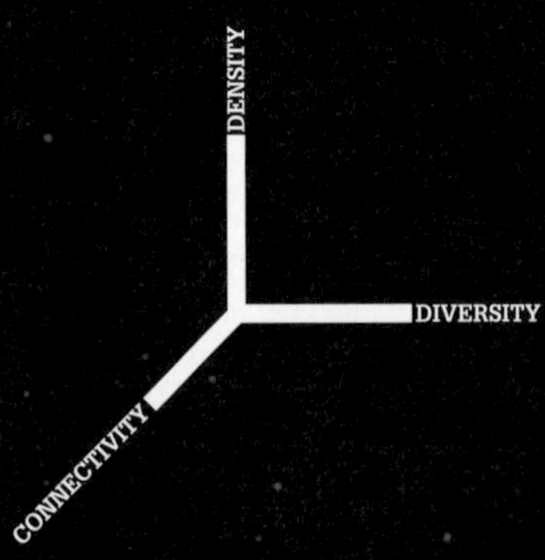

The World Class City Dimensions [fig. 2]

In a densely built city, diverse groups, spaces and activities exist in close proximity. This proximity generates interaction; it enhances awareness of individual and cultural differences.

A high-density city generates a compact, intensified, vivid cityscape; one that is vertically-oriented and three dimensional; and one with enough critical mass to support amenities and services near residential areas. High density has positive social effects; it tends to generate a sense of togetherness – of belonging to a community. High density intensifies the dynamics of a city, makes the use of its infrastructures efficient and increases the exchange of information, services and goods, globally as well as locally.

High density stimulates walking and biking. It reduces trip lengths and the use of public transport and therefore limits transport energy costs and carbon emissions. By delimiting a city's urban footprint, high density improves connectivity and helps to control unnecessary destruction of natural land and biodiversity. 'High density allows an increase in our capacities . . .' and it 'brings about the synergy of its components in environmental, economic, sociological, [political,] cultural and architectural terms.' [22]

Naturally, diversity – of ethnicity, race, culture, lifestyle – enriches urban life. [23] A diverse population generates intercultural exchange of ideas and knowledge; of customs and religious beliefs; of services and goods. A multicultural urban space encourages varied options for shopping, eating, leisure, recreation, education and working. In combination with urban density, diverse populations promote a healthy economy by generating restaurants, shops, bars, nightclubs, markets, cultural venues, festivals, recreational facilities and business districts. Urban diversity thus creates short- and long-term markets and enables micro- and macro-economies to flourish, generating creativity and creating diversified employment options.

UN-HABITAT emphasizes the importance of immigrants for cities in its report, *Migrants and Multicultural Cities: Problem or Possibility?*: 'Immigrants bring with them new ideas and strive to turn them into products of cultural consumption . . . and cities [need to] exploit these products and the spaces in which they [can be] sold, to promote their image'.[24] The world-class city strives to be a poly-ethnic entity with diverse and compelling architecture and programming. It is the duty of the world-class city to 'acknowledge and support the full diversity of all population groups.' The world-class city needs to develop 'a new, much more enlightened multicultural literacy.' [25] It therefore asks for supportive and integrative management; it 'should not be unilateral . . . [it] should include international, national and local bodies, all of which need to improve coordination and communication.' [26] When all social and ethnic groups participate in the governance and spatial production of the city, they help to nourish new forms of coexistence and to promote a diversified urban culture.

How to make all users of the city feel connected to their physical environment? How to support each resident's feeling of belonging to a certain global as well local community or neighbourhood?

The third dimension of the world-class city, *connectivity*[27], refers to the complex web of connections that mobilizes individuals, goods, information, agencies, institutions and other bodies globally, regionally and locally. This web includes communication and transportation networks, closed-cycle waste management, and air ventilation systems. It supports interaction and accessibility to and within the city, horizontally as well as vertically, and enhances the logic behind the city's layout and programmatic distribution. It provides the city with high-, mid- and low-speed systems to ensure the exchange of people, goods and information, generating new and improving old relationships.

The world-class city provides an efficient, reliable and well-integrated public transport system. Fast, well connected and easy-to-access transportation services eventually attract high net-worth visitors and investors to the city.

But regardless of public transport options, the world-class city is also a pedestrians' city – a city of neighbourhoods; a city where shops, schools, health centres, leisure and recreational facilities, and municipal administrative programs are within walking distance from residential areas. A world-class city enables its residents and visitors to move easily and comfortably throughout it within the shortest amount of time. This ease of circulation of people, goods and information has a positive effect on the economy of the city, conserving resources and precious space, boosting productivity and intelligence, and limiting the amount of time and money lost to pollution and congestion.

Synergistic Programming

'Successful places do not just provide one thing; rather they provide a range of quality of place options for different kinds of people at different stages in the life course.' [28]

Richard Florida

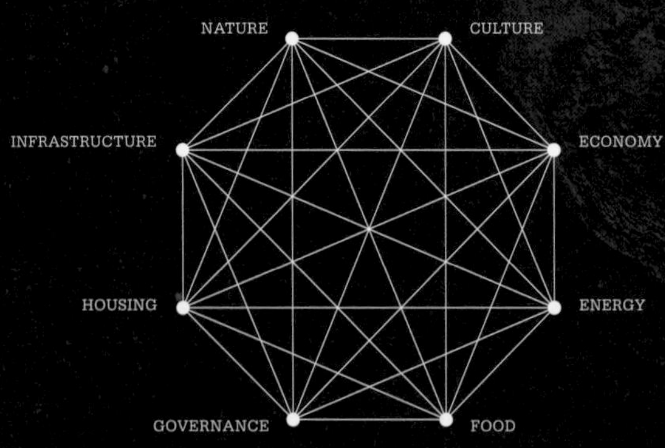

The World Class City Assessment Domains [fig. 3]

The vision of the world-class city is based on a vital, flexible urban environment where multiple functions and activities coexist. The architectural expressions of these functions need to be rewritten accordingly; such an integrative system asks for an adaptive architecture – one that embraces chaos, and is at the same time compelling and authentic; organized, functional and experimental; compact and accessible; rich in contrast, flexible, and above all, synergistic with other city programs.

The WCCF focuses on important criteria and performances of major domains of spatial city development. It aims to address all users of the city and the responsibilities of world-class development that come along with it. The WCCF, therefore, assists in providing a comprehensive evaluation and in clarifying issues of concern and long-term responsibilities in a time where population growth and resources are becoming increasingly scarce. Its task is to close the gap between exhaustion of our resources and our need to find living standards that fit the requirements of citizens.

The WCCF considers eight major domains in the assessment of world-class cities: culture, economy, energy, food, governance, housing, infrastructure and nature. [fig. 3] These domains form an interactive collective and define a dense, diverse and well-connected city – a city that enables vital urban and architectural production, and supports a healthy economy and lifestyle. These domains are synergistic; investment in one inherently reinforces the others.

Culture

Art and culture underpin the qualities of city life for individuals and communities. They help to generate the identity of a city, and contribute to the way that city projects itself, develops its profile, and competes in the regional, national and international arenas for investment. World-class cultural experience and public liveability find expression in a range of old streets, old buildings, houses of worship and trees, cultural buildings and amenities, including conference centres, museums, art galleries, cinemas, theatres, libraries, hotels, restaurants, leisure and recreational facilities, and public buildings; as well in a city's architecture, built form and public realm.

These historic streets and places, cultural venues and facilities contribute to the local and global identity of the city and are its motor for world-class branding. Their programs can catalyse architectural marvels, promoting modern as well as preserving historic landmarks.

An important objective for cities seeking world-class status is to identify areas that are suitable for the clustering and intensification of cultural activities and entertainment – live music, theatre, dance, street markets, dining and shopping. The concentration of these activities can encourage the rejuvenation of an area without compromising existing amenities. Proximity, accessibility and aesthetics need to be considered in order to attract local, regional and global users – or 'urban customers'.

Economy

The world-class city stimulates a diverse, free, stable and resilient economy, and offers all citizens the opportunity for rewarding and accessible work. A world-class free economy enables new markets and new developments that in return have a positive impact on its people's sense of 'being, belonging and becoming'. [29] It supports the informal sector by simplifying business permits and licenses and making them affordable, so that integration with the formal economy is possible for entrepreneurs of modest means.

World-class economy also supports development of an efficient, low-carbon

Key Objectives (Culture)

- Create multifunctional and vivid public spaces.
- Increase multiculturalism.
- Increase local and global newspapers for an adequate and diverse information exchange.
- Improve and intensify a diverse and accessible cultural program: cultural venues, performance venues, hotel/restaurant/ catering facilities, leisure and recreational facilities.
- Create effective meeting points in dense public areas.
- Facilitate high-quality services for elderly, families/children and the disabled.
- Offer a diverse range of affordable public and private services (retail, fresh food, utilities, information and advice), accessible to the entire community regardless of ethnic background.
- Encourage citizens to participate in the creation and programming of public cultural venues and activities.
- Create platforms for both high- and popular cultural events.
- Facilitate cultural venues that can accommodate both large and small audiences.
- Increase areas allocated to bazaars and street markets; encourage and authorize hawkers and small businesses to use these areas.
- Preserve cultural heritage.
- If waterfronts are available:
  1. Enlarge their promenades and make waterfront areas public.
  1.2. Connect waterfronts to nearby city clusters. Program waterfronts to facilitate small business opportunities that can be run by and for local residents.
- Enlarge recreational program by improving existing and adding new public parks, small businesses, marinas, beaches and other cultural amenities.
- Activate street life by offering a wide range of restaurants and cafés with in- and outdoor terraces.

economy that emphasizes use of sustainable resources and innovation in new green and sustainable technologies.

Energy

The world-class city must produce and control all of its own energy. It generates the electricity it needs with renewable energy sources. World-class energy is therefore based on a locally generated electricity system. These local generators use low- or zero-carbon fuels such as natural and renewable gasses. They are more efficient than big power stations because in addition to producing electricity, their waste heat can be used to heat buildings or, after conversion, to cool buildings. This combined system of cooling, heating and power is supportive to the closed cycle system and zero waste approach, and defines essential development criteria for the planning and construction of the world-class city. To minimize energy losses, this use of local, integrated energy supply asks for high urban density and a smart energy network grid.

Food

Can today's cities produce 100 per cent of their food supply within their own borders? Maybe not, but fundamental to world-class food supply is the creation of a new generation of farmers: city farmers. The integration of farming into the urban environment establishes a strong, immediate market and local awareness of food production among consumers. The world-class city is obliged to govern and financially support diversified local agricultural operations in order to increase the role of urban food production industries.

The world-class city creates infrastructures to support the processing and distribution of food products. It increases real estate planning assistance to

Key Objectives Economy

- Ensure financial viability by promoting economic activity through the participation of all citizens in the economic life of the city.
- Create fair and predictable regulatory frameworks that encourage commerce and investment, minimize transaction costs and legitimize the informal sector.
- Support informal economies.
- Attract diverse businesses and economic activity.
- Foster local-community based businesses and support large global businesses.

Key Objectives Energy

- Maximize use of renewable energies and achieve greater energy efficiency with focus on local production.
- Create smart cycles of renewable energy production.
- Reduce energy consumption.
- Establish an electricity network with reduced energy loss.
- Eliminate reliance on fossil fuels.
- Innovate on and create abundance of energy.

Key Objectives Food

- Minimize food miles by investing in local food production.
- Increase food control ensuring that all foods processed, prepared, stored, distributed and served at both retail and wholesale levels are safe and properly packaged.
- Link food production to other industries and domains of the city in order to support a zero-waste, closed-cycle system.
- Establish a large-scale urban farming industry.
- Support and encourage local urban farming.

farmers and food industries. For the world-class city, it is a necessary challenge and responsibility to mix housing, shopping and commerce with farming and food processing industries. This mixing helps to reduce food miles, increase food control and reuse energies that are freed in the food production cycle.

Governance

A good city can only be made and maintained with a good city government – one that ensures equity for all communities, particularly those prone to poverty and social exclusion. Such a government promotes cultural, ethnic, religious and racial diversity and encourages every citizen to participate in the ongoing creation of the city. [30] It encourages the formation of independent associations or public agencies in order to create an active platform on public issues, needs and desires. Good urban governance therefore stimulates all citizens to participate in the programming and construction of their city.

Housing

As one of the most important spatial aspects of the world-class city, the housing domain should provide all citizens with a well-located, connected, functional, comfortable and affordable private living space in proximity to social and administrative amenities of the city. The world-class city develops local plans to diversify its housing production and increase its housing accessibility and adaptability. It preserves, maintains and upgrades the existing housing stock, and creates possibilities to add new housing in order to increase dwelling space per capita and support rehabilitation of neighbourhoods and growth. A world-class housing program encourages the production of customized and accessory apartments and houses to stimulate a flexible and diverse housing market.

Key Objectives Governance

- Maintain political stability.
- Improve civil liberty and free choice.
- Increase transparency and reduce bureaucracy.
- Empower citizens and increase participation in creation of the city.
- Ensure that women and men have equal access to decision-making processes, resources and basic services and that this access is measured through gender disaggregated data.
- Commit to poverty reduction.
- Eliminate censorship.
- Eliminate corruption of business and government.

Key Objectives Housing

- Provide all citizens with access to good quality, well-located and affordable housing.
- Offer a diverse range of housing typologies that address the needs and desires of customers in regard to space, layout, percentage of daylight, ventilation, location, views, indoor and outdoor spaces, etc.
- Incorporate outdoor spaces such as balconies and patios into the design. These elements are of high importance and will boost the quality of living.
- Provide housing designed for maximum comfort.
- Diversify housing typologies.
- Promote social cohesion by mixing households of different income groups and ethnic backgrounds.
- Upgrade and renovate housing stock on a regular basis.

Infrastructure

Basic infrastructural networks and services such as drinking water, sanitation, electricity, communication systems, waste management, public transport and smooth traffic routes for people, goods and information are essential for a pleasant, successful and functional city environment. Without comfortable and fast transportation, a city is likely to fall short in its standard of living, and will fail to attract important investors. The world-class city needs to be multi-directionally connected – globally, regionally and locally. In other words: world-class transportation is based on a multi-modal system addressing both high- and low-speed networks. These networks make the city dynamic and accessible to residents, as well as to tourists and business travellers.

In addition, the world-class city provides all citizens with an affordable, high-speed communication network to expand the scope of digital interaction with citizens and businesses within the city and abroad. For the world-class city it is important to make uncensored voice and data services available to all citizens and businesses in order to enhance local, regional and global digital connectedness, and to improve information exchange.

A world-class city infrastructure advocates a smart, zero-waste management system that supports recycling and closed waste cycles and eliminates other pollutants of air, water and soil.

Nature

The world-class city can be a living biotope that counteracts the depletion of natural and arable lands and the massive extinction of animals and plants caused by urban sprawl. In addition to improvements in air, water and soil quality, world-class nature development increases local capacity for larger open green space acquisition and enables a mix of green attributes within dense urban public spaces. The world-class city limits the

Key Objectives Infrastructure

a. Transportation

- Improve pedestrian and bicycle access.
- Integrate poorly connected neighbourhoods.
- Increase international airport capacity.
- Maximize accessibility for all people in and around the city as well as international migrants.
- Increase use of sustainable transport modes (public transport, walking, cycling, etc.)
- Accelerate developments of a multi-modal transportation system with both: high- and low speed connections.
- Enhance overall accessibility through additional public transport links.
- Improve 'walkability' by enlarging pedestrian walkways and adding street-level crossings, footbridges and subway access.

b. Communication

- Improve information and communications technologies.
- Ensure adequate internet connectivity.
- Make digital channels affordable and available to all citizens.
- Increase number of WiFi hotspots.

c. Waste Management and Sanitation

- Achieve zero municipal waste.
- Invest in recycling and closed waste cycles.
- Minimize production of waste across all sectors and encourage re-use, recycling, remanufacturing and recovery rates.
- Invest in smart waste management systems.
- Eliminate volumes of solid waste in landfills.
- Implement a smart waste-to-energy management system to eliminate landfills and generate electricity.
- Implement community, street- and park-cleaning services to minimize litter in neighbourhoods, open spaces and recreational areas.
- Enforce rules to eliminate domestic-, construction- and building waste-dumping.

proliferation of urban sprawl through densification and intensification of the built urban landscape, and the smart incorporation of nature and animal life within the city's architectural domain.

By supporting necessary ecologies and conditions, the world-class city aims to foster the coexistence of plants, insects, animals and humans within a dense urban environment.

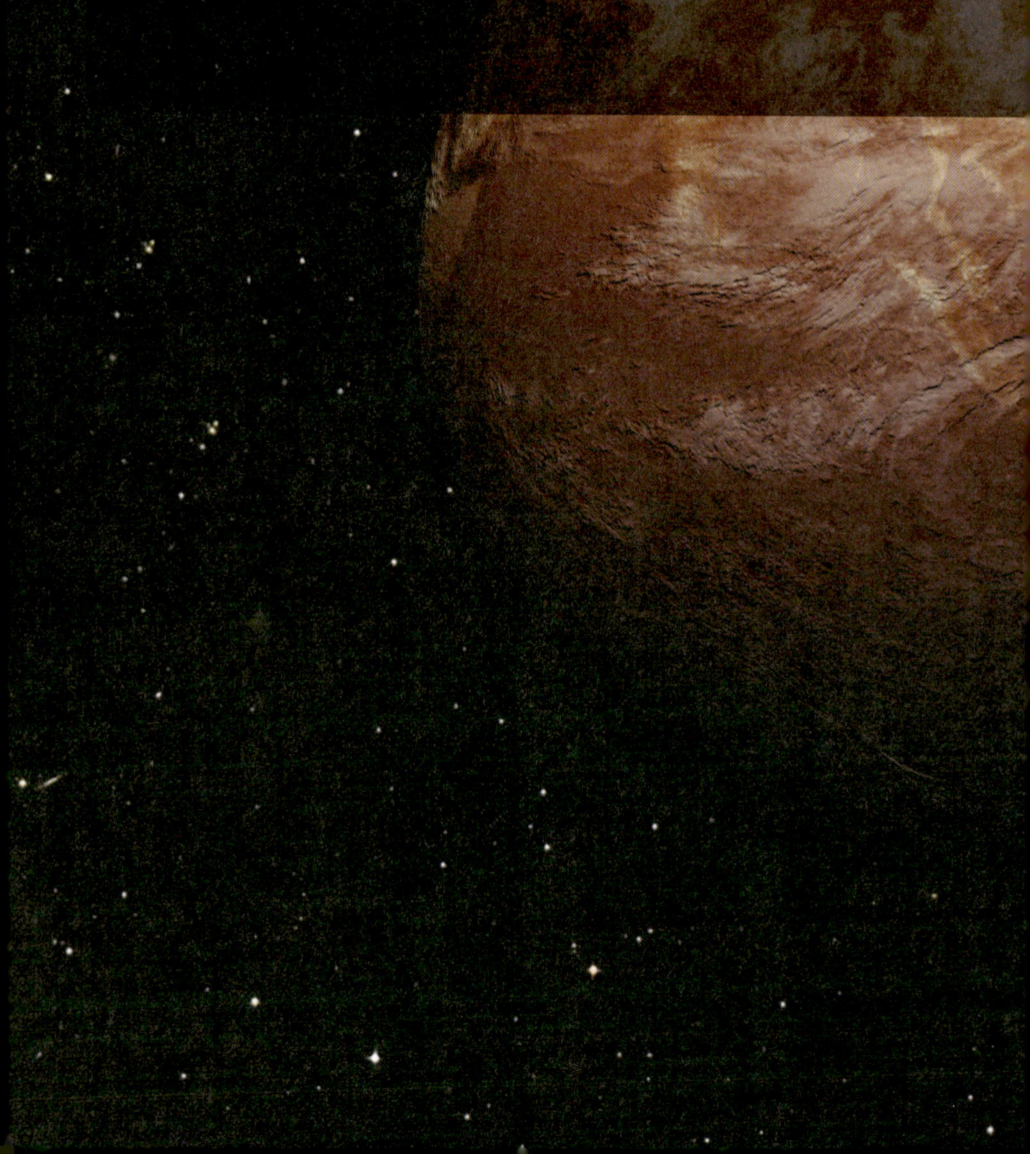

Key Objectives Nature

a. Transportation
- Improve pedestrian and bicycle access.
- Integrate poorly connected neighbourhoods.

a. Biodiversity
- Increase and enhance biodiversity by intensifying mountains and wetlands, and by adding architecture that provides shelter for animals and insects.
- Protect, enhance, facilitate and promote natural biodiversity.
- Sustain the number of species in the city.
- Provide architecture that attracts new species and nourishes and restores diverse living systems.
- Increase vegetation in public spaces.
- Protect and enhance natural open green space.
- Maximize access to green areas and provide adequate recreational facilities for all residents and visitors.

b. Air Quality
- Reduce smog levels by increasing airflow.
- Improve air quality.
- Reduce urban heat islands.

c. Water Quality
- Improve water quality.
- Protect and enhance water bodies.

d. Soil Quality
- Regenerate contaminated land.

How World-Class is Hong Kong?

Dream-City of Contrasts

'To realise our vision of Hong Kong as a world-class city with a thriving economy and an affluent and culturally rich society, it is first and foremost necessary to cultivate and retain a critical mass of talented people.' [31]

Tung Chee Hwa

Hong Kong is ranked third as a global financial centre (Global Financial Cities Index, Z/Yen Group, 2010) [fig.4], fifth as global city (Global Cities Index, Foreign Police Magazine, 2010) [fig. 5], and an embarrassing 71st for its living conditions (Quality of Living Index, Mercer, 2010) [fig. 6].

According to the Cost of Living Index (Economist Intelligence Unit, 2010) Hong Kong is an unaffordable city, and, based on current trends, its cost of living is still rising. [fig. 7] Hong Kong also scores poorly on the education index, suggesting that too many of its residents are unable to read and write. [fig. 8] [32]
But Hong Kong has more to offer – world-class qualities that these rankings don't measure. It is a dream-city of contrasts – stunning skyscrapers and magnificent nature; shopping and mountains; a comfortable climate, metropolis and beach, Ironically, Hong Kong's insularity has enabled it to flourish. Hong Kong – almost – has it all.

As one of the most compact, densely built cities in the world, with close to 30,000 people per square kilometre of built-up land, Hong Kong has a stupendous skyline; nowhere else can you find more than 3000

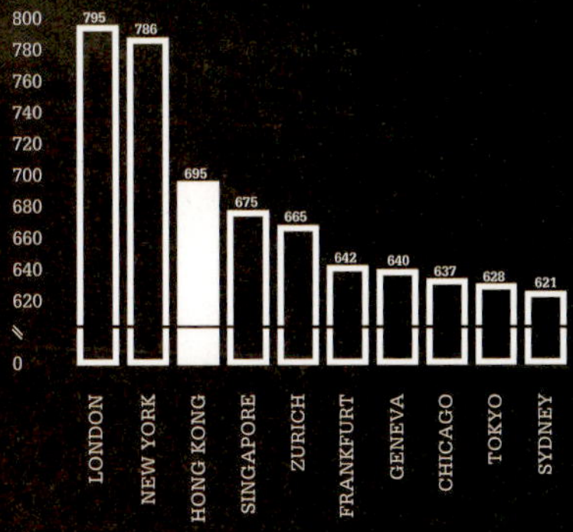

score calculated by a factor assessment model

Global Financial Centers Index [fig. 4]

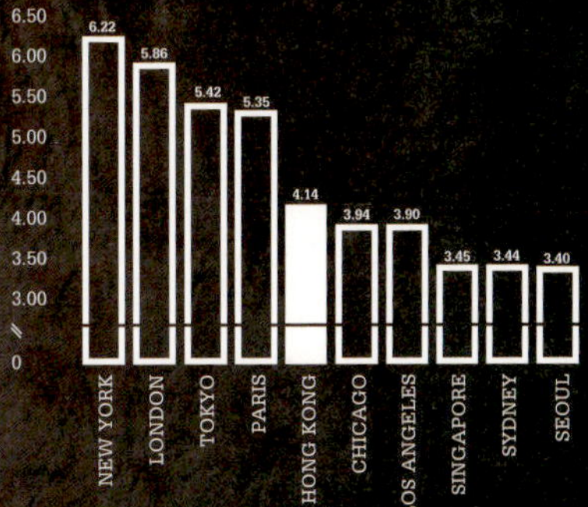

scores are computed as a weighted abstraction of 25 metrics across five dimensions

Global Cities Index [fig. 5]

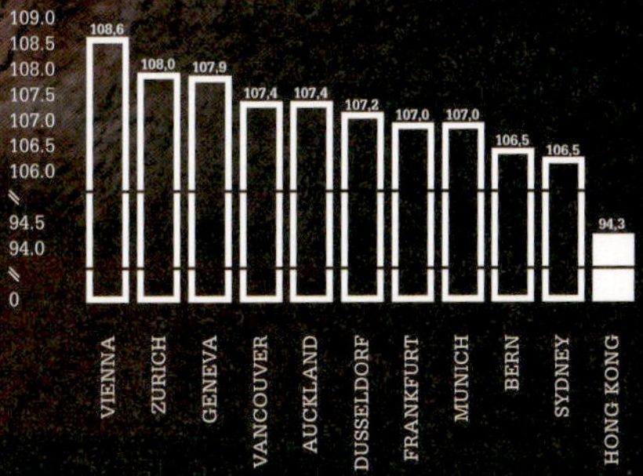

scores are computed as a weighted abstraction, Base City is New York, US (=100), (data hong kong: 2008, ranked 70)

Quality of living Index [fig. 6]

buildings over 90 m tall. [fig. 9] Even New York City – which for decades was known as the world's leading skyscraper city with 882 buildings over 90 m tall – is dwarfed by Hong Kong.
Such a density-driven mindset could lead to new types of public and private developments and boost urban creativity and a world-class lifestyle.

Many claim that Hong Kong has no space to extend – that new developments would threaten its nature and waterfronts. In fact the opposite is true. Hong Kong has plenty of space to build. Restrictions due to territorial borders have always generated inventive solutions in Hong Kong; why not now? First, the city has to break its habit of land reclamation – especially at the waterfront along Victoria Harbour – to accommodate its new developments and avoid dropping real estate prices. Instead, the existing urban envelope could become even more densely built. Several areas are ripe for development: the former airport is waiting for a new life; the harbour ports can be extended or moved

Culture

Compared to other world cities like London, Paris, New York and Shanghai, cultural activity is sparse in Hong Kong; there are almost no operas [fig. 10], only a handful of museums [fig. 11] and few theatres [fig. 12] or cinemas. [fig. 13] Instead, shopping is the main attraction. Nowhere on the planet is there such a high concentration of retail space. According to many tourists and online forums, the experience of shopping in Hong Kong is considered one of the best and most varied in Asia, ranging from bargain alleys and factory outlets, to huge malls, to exclusive designer boutiques. Despite the abundance and variety of products available in Hong Kong, shopping-area developers have overlooked comfort and convenience. Where cities like Shanghai [33] and Singapore [34] invest in the 'pedestrianization' of their cities, Hong Kong seems to have forgotten the importance of providing 'walkable' and attractive shopping

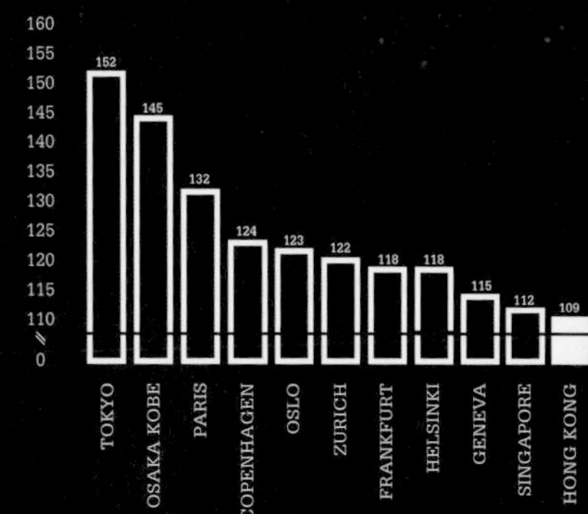

Cost of Living Index [fig. 7]

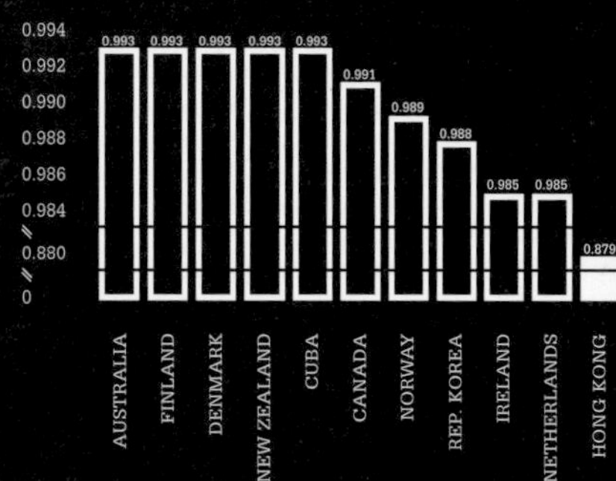

computed scores are based on data on adult literacy rates and gross enrolment ratios

Education Index [fig. 8]

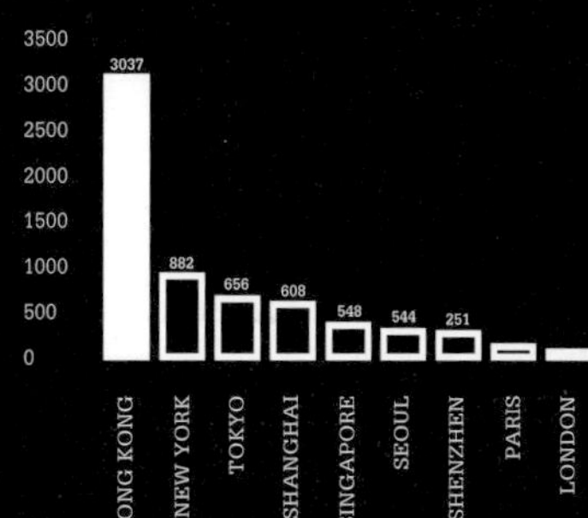

Amount of Buildings >90 meter [fig. 9]

streets. Its sidewalks are cracked and user-unfriendly; its shopping areas are interiorized and difficult to access
on foot. Singapore [34] invest in the 'pedestrianization' of their cities, Hong Kong seems to have forgotten the importance of providing 'walkable' and attractive shopping streets. Its sidewalks are cracked and user-unfriendly; its shopping areas are interiorized and difficult to access on foot.

Economy

Since the opening of the new territories, the competition with other cities in the region, especially the 'four S's' – Shenzhen, Shanghai, Singapore and Seoul – has left its marks. Shenzhen, Singapore, Shanghai and Seoul are claiming Hong Kong's position at the leading port in Southeast Asia. [fig. 14] [fig. 15] Hong Kong is deemed to be the region's only 'international' financial centre; nonetheless Shenzhen and Shanghai are taking over the region's financial services and stock market activities. [fig. 16]
According to a 2001 study by the Heritage Foundation, individuals in Hong Kong are freer than those in any other city to work, produce, consume and invest as they choose. Since 1995, Hong Kong's economy has been unsurpassed as the freest on the planet, closely followed by Singapore. [fig. 17]

In recent decades, the production of many goods has moved to other parts of the Pearl River Delta. With Guangzhou claiming Hong Kong's former position as the new centre of manufacturing in the Pearl River Delta region, the label 'Made in Hong Kong' has nearly vanished. Alternatively, Hong Kong's service sector has gained prominence in its economy, claiming 92 per cent of its total GDP in 2008 and employing 88 per cent of the total labour force. [35]
Hong Kong has long been described as the most lucrative gateway for foreign enterprises that seek to enter markets in mainland China.

With its economic policies of free enterprise and free trade (no import

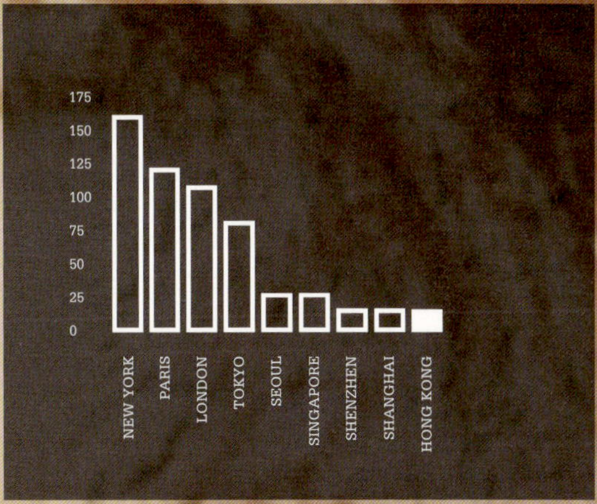

Number of Operas [fig. 10]

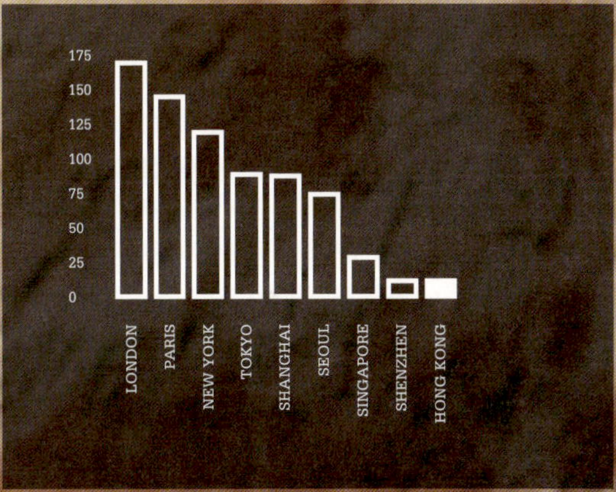

Number of Museums [fig. 11]

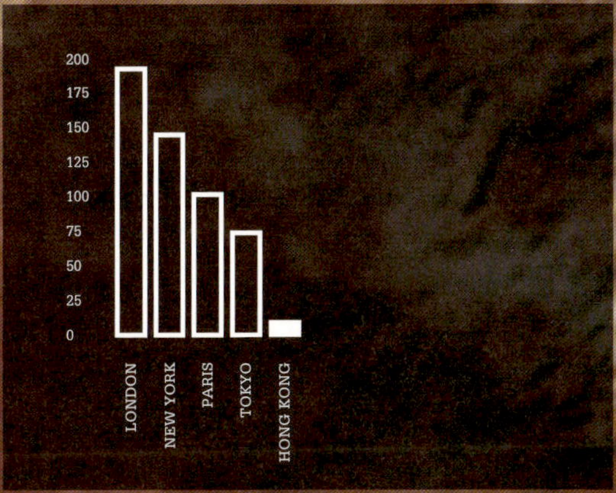

Number of Theaters [fig. 12]

tariffs), and with English as its main language, Hong Kong has become an economic playground. But nowadays, Shanghai and Shenzhen are attracting international enterprises with their new infrastructures, trading centres, and similar free-trading and low-tax conditions. [fig. 17] Shanghai in particular has become Hong Kong's main rival in the battle to be the international gateway to China's mainland market.

Energy

Hong Kong's use of energy is inefficient and lacks focus on renewable resources. In fact, Hong Kong imports more energy than any entity on the planet: 42 billion megawatt hours per year, which is 99.72 per cent of its total energy supply. [fig. 18] In the office sector, up to 48 per cent of the total energy consumption is spent solely on air conditioning.
The city is highly dependent on available resources and fluctuating market prices. But Hong Kong's compactness and geographical location make it suited to create smart cycles of renewable energy production and establish an electricity network with reduced energy loss. In addition to minimizing its energy consumption the city could achieve greater energy efficiency by focusing on local renewable energy production.

Food

Hong Kong's use of energy is inefficient and lacks focus on renewable resources. In fact, Hong Kong imports more energy than any entity on the planet: 42 billion megawatt hours per year, which is 99.72 per cent of its total energy supply. [fig. 18] In the office sector, up to 48 per cent of the total energy consumption is spent solely on air conditioning.

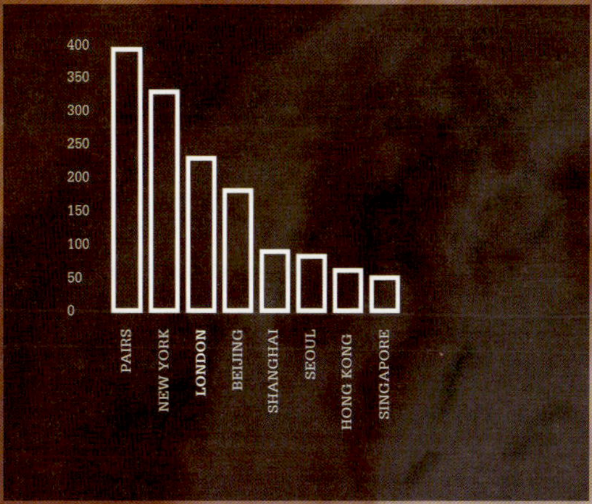

Number of Cinemas [fig. 13]

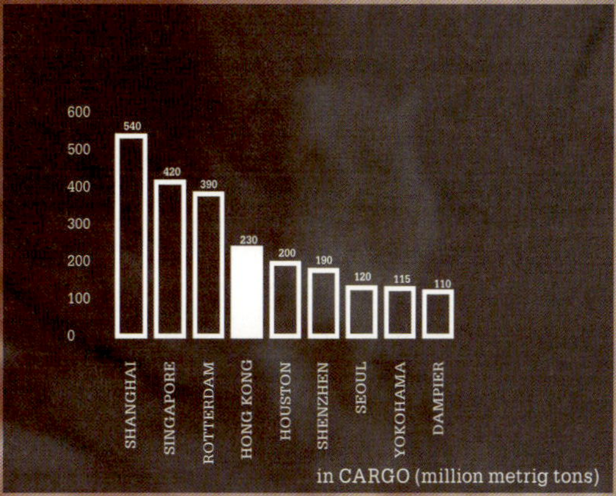

Largest Seaports of the World [fig. 14]

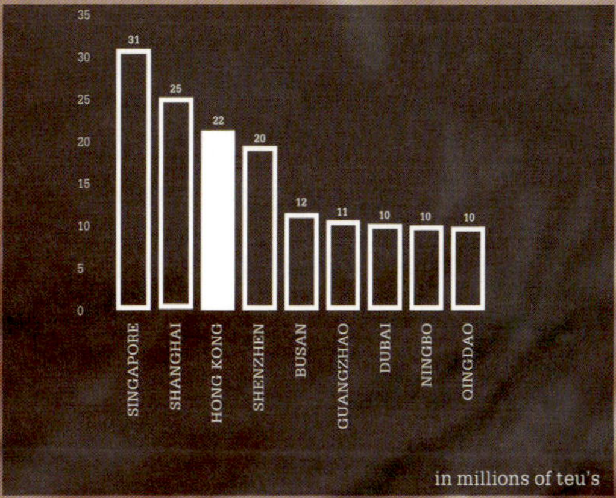

Largest Containerport of the World [fig. 15]

The city is highly dependent on available resources and fluctuating market prices. But Hong Kong's compactness and geographical location make it suited to create smart cycles of renewable energy production and establish an electricity network with reduced energy loss. In addition to minimizing its energy consumption the city could achieve greater energy efficiency by focusing on local renewable energy production.

Governance

Hong Kong (as Macau) has been a Special Administrative Region (SAR) of China since the British handed back this colony to the Chinese rule in 1997. These SAR's have been established and constituted in 1982 by the British and China. Compared to other typical Chinese administrations Hong Kong's is 'special' due to its national sovereignty, high-degree autonomy and the freedoms of religion, expression and of assembly.
Hong Kong has a powerful government that wants to display its dominance through large-scale projects. These projects are the most visible accomplishments and tend to reflect the City Government's desire in becoming a vigorous and prosperous city.

The Hong Kong government's budget is relatively high compared to other Chinese Cities. Its dominance is strong but the social forces are weak. [37] The government carefully listens to stakeholders and care about economic surpluses in the development of their city, but it shows very limited involvement of citizens and their participation in the creation of their city. The government seems to have limited compassion with its citizens and its history. Thus, full democracy needs serious attention and still to be executed. In addition, the value of old streets, old trees, old temples and its colonial architecture need to be recognized as valuable not solely by its citizens, and need recognition, a conservation and regeneration plan by the government in order to have the cultural diversity of Hong Kong properly and

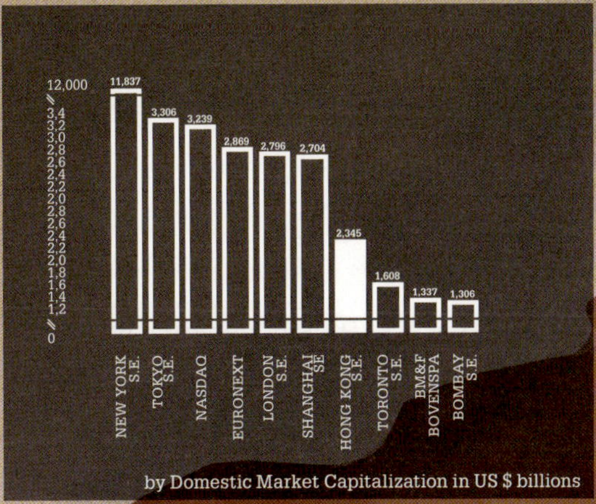

World's Stock Exchanges [fig. 16]

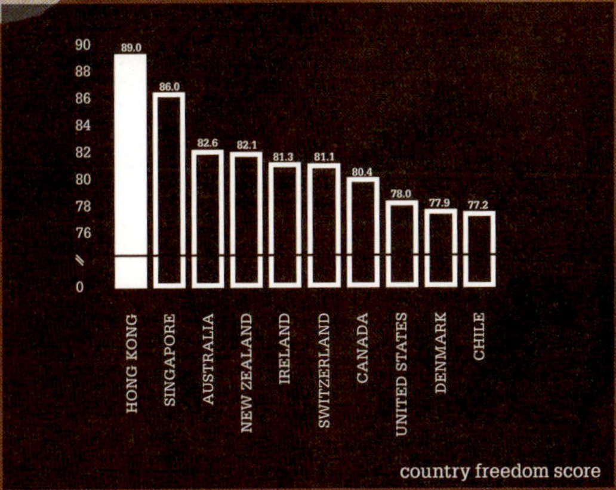

Economic Freedom Index [fig. 17]

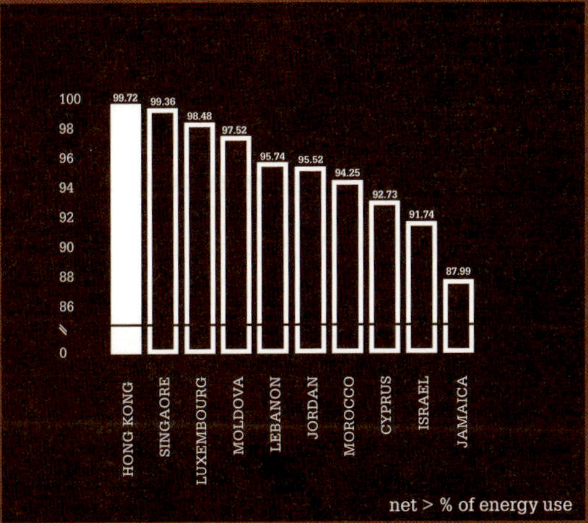

Energy Imports [fig. 18]

proudly expressed. The government needs a strong vision for Hong Kong that includes the creative energy of all its stakeholders.

Housing

The land prices in Hong Kong are amongst the highest in the world, averaging 1200 euros per square metre. Real estate prices are also astronomical: In 2010, the average mid-level apartment of 120 m^2 sold for about 12,200 euros per square metre, while apartments of 200 m^2 in upper-class neighbourhoods like Victoria Peak were worth about 4.3 million euros, with a square metre price of over 21,300 euros. [38] As housing prices continue to rise, opportunities diminish for Hong Kongers with a median monthly household income of 1670 euros to purchase an apartment or house. [39]

The rental prices in the private market, which comprises half of the rental market, are relatively high as a consequence of a policy that allows landlords to freely negotiate rental prices within the private sector. Although the rental market is dominated by the profit-oriented free market, the public housing sector is relatively large in Hong Kong, renting out about 30 per cent of the total 2.3 million homes. In the 1950s, dwelling space averaged only 2.23 square metres per person. Today, with an average of about 10 m^2 per capita across all households, Hong Kong's apartments are miniscule compared to those in cities like Singapore (32 m^2 per capita), or even Tokyo (15 m^2 per capita). [fig. 20] [40] Despite improvements since the 1950s, many of Hong Kong's residents, especially of the middle class, are disappearing to Shenzhen where they can find more spacious, attractive and affordable places to live. Hong Kong needs to increase its available dwelling space per capita by 300 per cent in order to be ranked among those cities that offer an average of 30 square meters per person. In addition, by diversifying its housing market the city could stimulate a more socially mixed society and use its waterfronts more for housing developments.

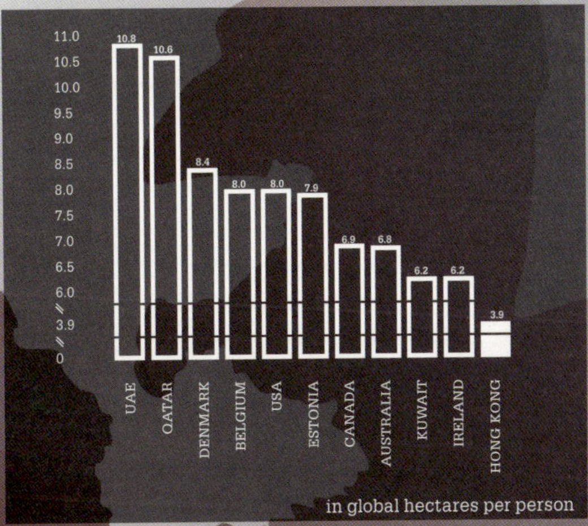

Ecological Footprint [fig. 19]

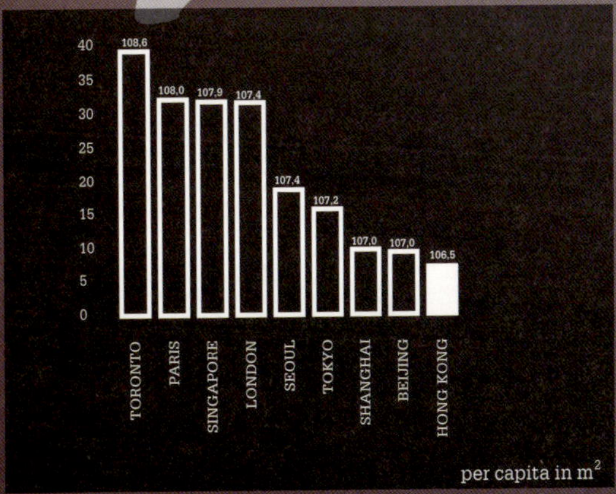

Dwelling Space [fig. 20]

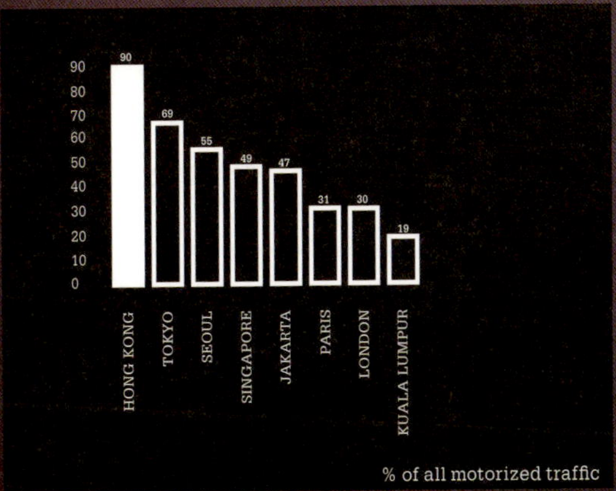

Public Transport [fig. 21]

and heavily used on the planet. In a city with a very few privately owned vehicles – only 400,000 among its total population of seven million – subways, trams, trains, busses and ferries make up 89 per cent of the city's total motorized urban transportation. [fig. 21] Hong Kong's railway system counts over 30 million passengers per urban rail line mile. [fig. 22] Hong Kong's network for slow-speed transportation needs radical improvement; specifically, its streets need to be made attractive and functional for walking and biking.
Hong Kong also has a poor waste management system that scatters too many landfills across the city, blocking precious land from valuable development.

Nature

Hong Kong has the world's highest percentage of urban green space, with over 80 per cent of its territory comprised of mountains and vast wetlands. [fig. 23] Hong Kong's diverse ecosystems generate impressive biodiversity including '3000 varieties of flowering plants and trees, over 2000 moth-, 110 dragonfly- and 230 butterfly species. Hong Kong hosts one third of the total bird species in China, and an array of freshwater fish, amphibians, reptiles and mammals.' [41]
In addition, Hong Kong has more than 700 km of coastline. Much of this property is suited for recreational use and other waterfront development. [fig. 24][42]

Although Hong Kong contains large green spaces – its mountains – in the heart of the city, its recreational and green zones are neglected, largely underused and underdeveloped; its public green spaces are practically nonexistent. Despite moderate activity on its fabulous white sand beaches, the many country Parks in the North Eastern New Territories are nearly forgotten. The hills, forests and parks are poorly programmed and difficult to reach; often, they appear to be practically abandoned.

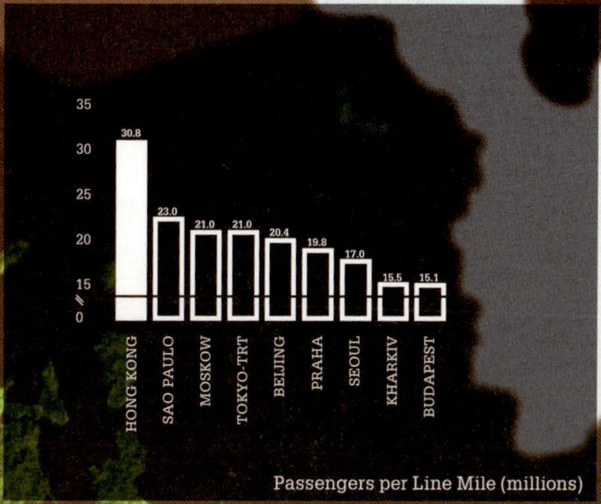

Urban Rail per City Nation index [fig. 22]

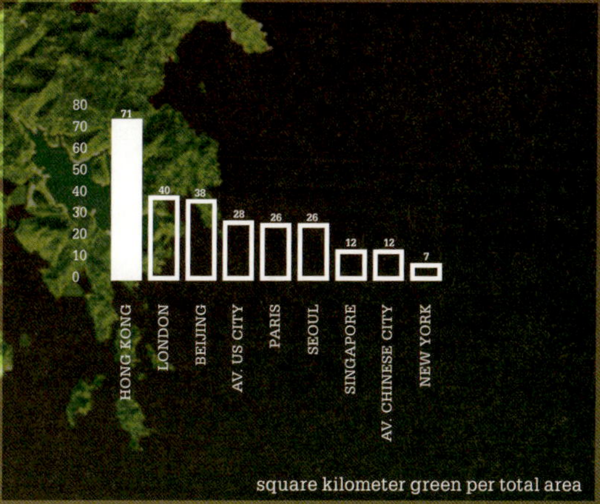

Green Space [fig. 23]

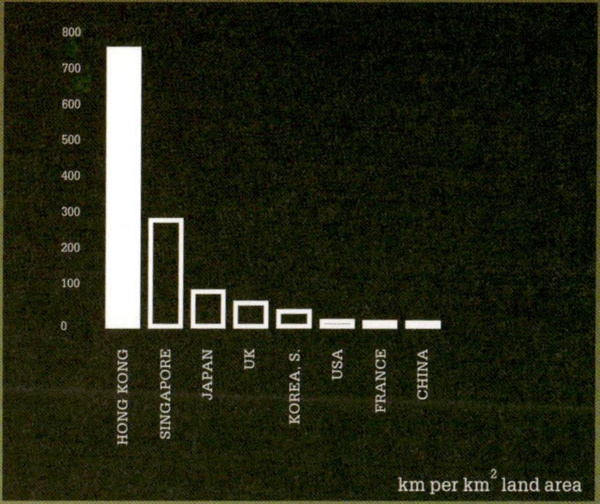

Coastline Index [fig. 24]

Investment Strategies for Hong Kong

Hong Kong: A Benchmark for World-Class

'To be a World Class City means that we should be a world leader. This competitive advantage will make Hong Kong a truly World Class City where no other city can match.' [43]

Tony M. W. Kwok

Although its portfolio is still thin and its performance falls short in many domains, Hong Kong has the potential to become a benchmark for the world-class city by offering not simply a remarkable skyline, but, more importantly, a desirable lifestyle. Hong Kong can make a comeback if it invests inthe qualities that make it – and have made it – exceptional.

Hong Kong could cultivate its assets in order to stimulate creativity and become an experimental playground for world-class development. But how? Can Hong Kong benefit from its relatively free economic environment, good urban governance, its high density and its global and local connectedness?

Although Hong Kong has constructed a series of remarkable buildings, most are mediocre. Why? Does its culture somehow resist quality? Are there regulations that obstruct the process of qualifying good design? Hong Kong deserves a special type of architecture: one that exploits and enhances the relation of its dense urban texture to its green and lush nature.

If Hong Kong aspires to world-class status, it's got some work to do. The city can only remain competitive if its strengths are reinforced, its weaknesses improved. The city's transformation will require a clear and cohesive plan, and the commitment of all stakeholders and authorities involved. An analysis of Hong Kong's qualities through the lens of The Why Factory's World-Class City Framework defines a series of investment strategies for the domains that need reinforcement. Although, investment strategies for Governance and Economy are powerful and fundamental for the achievement of world-class status, they are not addressed in this study because their political focus on policies and regulations have an indirect influence on spatial developments. Nevertheless, the Hong Kong City Government, the Economical Affairs Council and its main partners need to make Hong Kong more democratic and support its informal economies, and more importantly, encourage inhabitants and local talents to get more involved in the creation of their city.
Without these investments, Hong Kong will not only lose its leading position as a global financial centre, it will also miss the opportunity to become an exemplary world-class city.

Invest in Culture

Hong Kong has a poor cultural package; its landscape is dominated by oversized-malls, monotonous shopping miles and restaurants. This single-minded production of commerce has been the mission of insensitive city governance and profit-oriented real estate developers, not the people of Hong Kong. Unfortunately, investments like these do little to express the lively cultural personality of Hong Kong and its citizens.

How could Hong Kong stimulate world-class cultural activity? How could it preserve its historical cultural heritage? Could the arts claim a significant position in Hong Kong's public life? What kind of architecture would this 'city of culture' require?

Sky Corridors

Imagine a system of horizontal connectors, or sky corridors penetrating Hong Kong's vertical landscape! Suddenly, the city is more compact, more three-dimensional supporting a vivid horizontal movement on multiple levels.

These corridors can be programmed to generate an animated web of cultural activity, while linking important locations as, historical sites, ancient streets, old buildings and artistic villages.

Filled with galleries, cinemas, theatres, museums, ateliers and artists' residences, and integrating shops supporting the informal economy, hotels, offices, and restaurants, they attract mainstream

audiences as well as more specialized groups. Hong Kong becomes a social, accessible, attractive and 'walkable' city.

Day and night, this concentrated mix of culture, work, housing and leisure activates, intensifies and diversifies Hong Kong's public life.

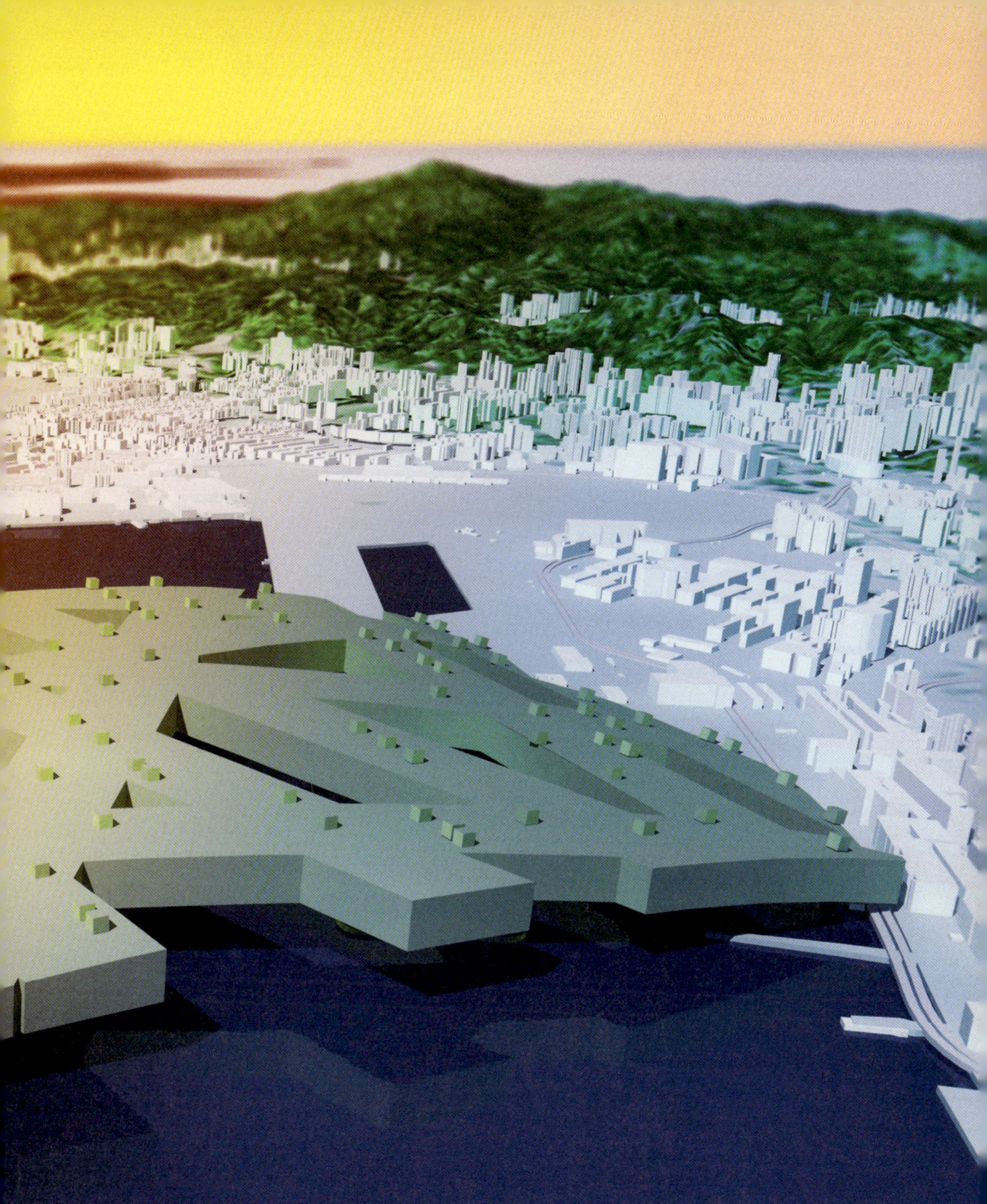

Culture Bridge

Can a bridge serve as both a connector and a destination? Can it carry program, in addition to linking program?

Envision a new central plaza spanning the water between Kowloon Peninsula and Hong Kong Island – an iconic regional culture-hub.

This monumental landmark houses theatres, operas, cinemas, nightclubs and art galleries. No longer do people visit Hong Kong only to shop.

Finally, the arts have become a major attraction. Hong Kong might even evolve into Southeast Asia's cultural centre.

Sunken Culture

Could an underground knot of cultural program also serve an infrastructural purpose? Could culture 'open' the water and reintegrate the city?

Building new dams in the bay creates valleys
connecting the two most important city parts. Huge
walls cut through the water, with waterfalls

streaming over them; they help to reorient the city-centre towards its revitalized waterfronts. Aqueducts spanning the new valleys enable boats

and fish to cross. New subway stations and tunnels are built to ensure its accessibility.

This sunken cultural hub is Hong Kong's newest attraction and ultimate icon.

Invest in Energy

How can Hong Kong supply more, or even all, of its own energy? In its pursuit of world-class status, Hong Kong urgently needs to invest in renewable energy production and reduce its fossil fuel-based energy consumption. Cities with such high energy demands need to take responsibility for providing their own resources.

Venetian Hong Kong

In the dense areas of Hong Kong, building mass, traffic and poor ventilation cause the city to heat up. What if Hong Kong built canals and tunnels?

They would limit automobile pollution and create cooling buffers that drastically reduce the energy consumed by air conditioning- and ventilation

systems in densely populated or closed-off areas. Imagine this new Venetian element in Hong Kong's cityscape. Imagine this new Venetian element in Hong Kong's cityscape. Waterways pervade dense

central areas; 'exotic' public transport options, like water taxis, are introduced. Inner city neighbourhoods become more attractive, with car-free zones, enhanced 'walkability' and increased real estate values.

central areas; 'exotic' public transport options, like water taxis, are introduced. Inner city neighbourhoods become more attractive, with

car-free zones, enhanced 'walkability' and increased real estate values.

Energy Islands

What if Hong Kong could produce its own energy? Could the city even reverse its current pattern, and turn energy into an export product? In this fantasy, Hong Kong cashes in on its

favourable conditions for solar radiation. No more cumbersome equipment squeezed onto small rooftops; instead solar power plants float elegantly in the bays, like water lilies. These islands do more

than fulfil energy demands; they create new possibilities for recreation and educational activities. Using a surface area of only 40 square kilometres, Hong Kong can supply its own annual energy in this

manner. But this area is a mere 2.4 per cent of a body of water measuring 1800 km^2. That leaves 1760 km^2 of water to accommodate even more energy islands and generate a surplus.

Using a surface area of only 40 square kilometres, Hong Kong can supply its own annual energy in this manner. But this area is a mere 2.4 per cent of a body of water measuring 1800 km2. That leaves 1760 km^2 of water to accommodate even more energy islands and generate a surplus.

By exploiting this opportunity, Hong Kong can sell green energy to neighbouring cities and mainland China, and become the world's largest and most attractive solar energy city.

Invest in Food

Food yields are declining worldwide, especially those of rice and cereals due to rain, hail, drought, pests, etc. Hong Kong is almost fully dependent on the import of meat, fish and agricultural goods. Can the city take responsibility for its own food production and expand its agricultural domain? The city could introduce large farming areas, food distribution centres and local farmers markets. By prioritizing urban food production and city farms, Hong Kong could provide social,economic, health and environmental benefits. By participating in community gardens, Hong Kongers come into contact with the sources of their food.

Urban food production generates important local awareness of our food consumption habits and creates opportunities for socio-economic growth. In addition, urban food production could lead to large savings on energy and logistics. Households, offices and other industries could benefit from these local food factories as they could be linked to plants that produce biogas and electricity.

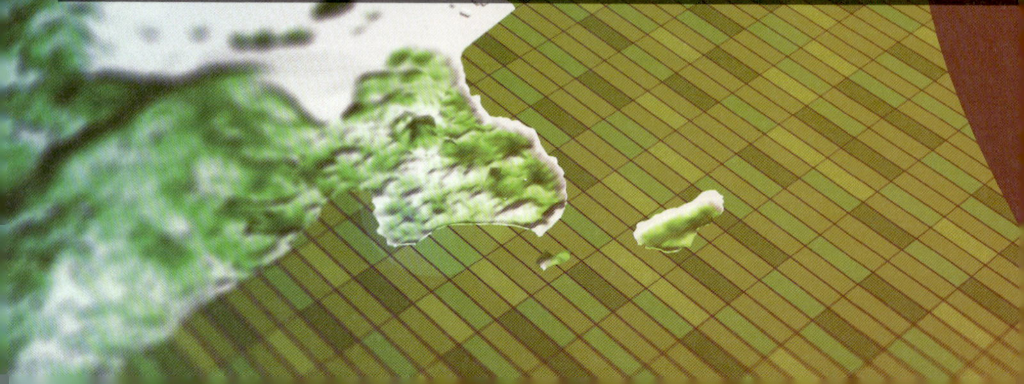

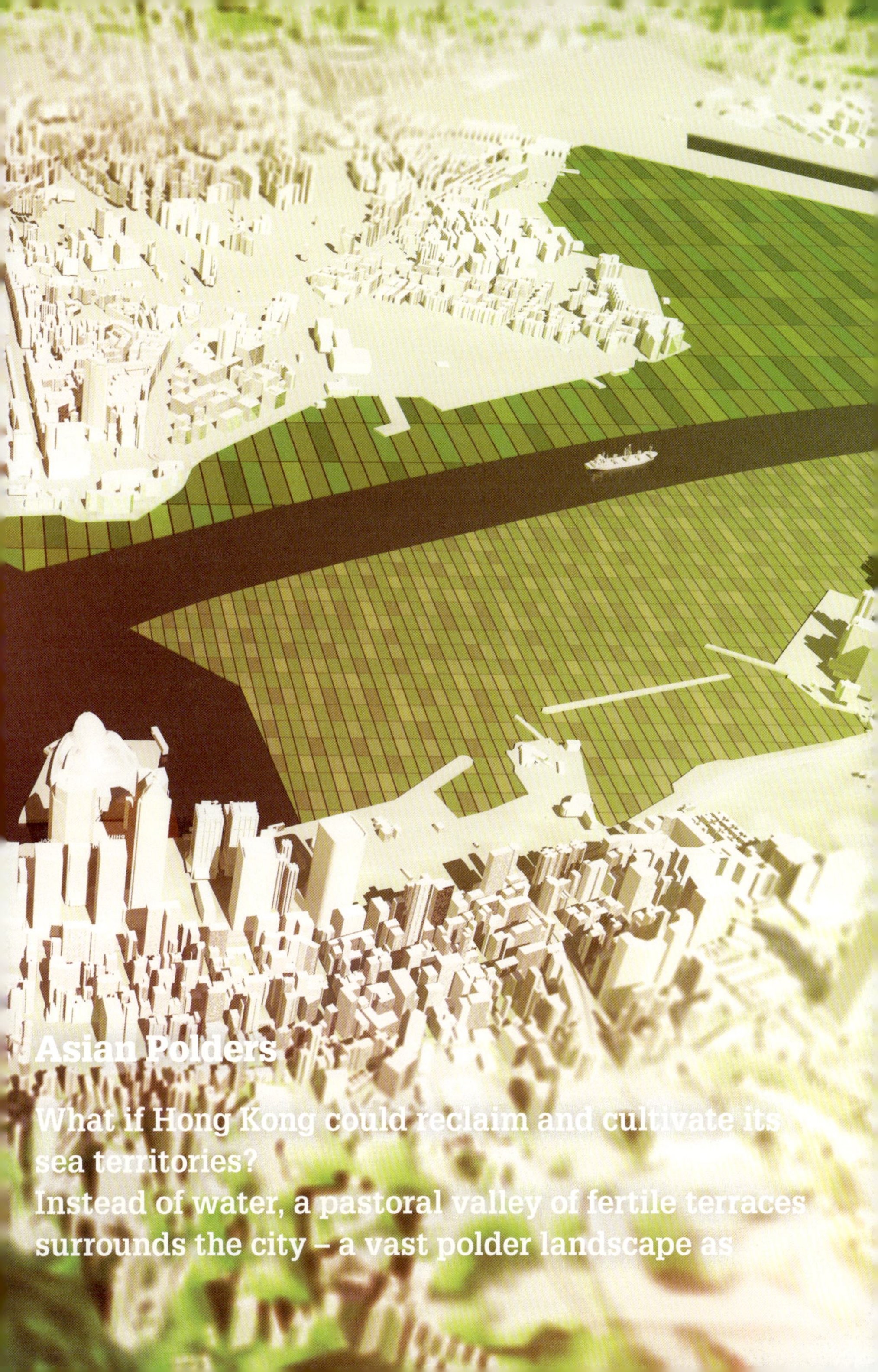

Asian Polders

What if Hong Kong could reclaim and cultivate its sea territories?
Instead of water, a pastoral valley of fertile terraces surrounds the city – a vast polder landscape as

backdrop for urban expansion. Hong Kong becomes autarkic in its food production!
No longer is the city dependent on imports. Instead, the primary ingredients of certain food products are

produced within city limits, generating an entire new industry. Shorter production and transportation lines cause a decrease in mass food transportation, reducing congestion of interregional traffic systems.

Food Pillars

A world-class Hong Kong produces its food in greenhouses that use new technologies, like

hydroponic farming, decreasing the city's ecological footprint by a third.

Stacking these greenhouses further diminishes the footprint in the area.

By producing all food in one central, optimized, easy-to-regulate location, the city creates its own food

hub with distribution lines that correspond directly to its population's needs.

Invest in Housing

As a result of high land prices and strict regulations, Hong Kong's population lives in what are close to the smallest houses in the world. The limitations on housing have halted potential growth, discouraged diversity and blocked innovation. In search of better quality housing, the middle class is escaping to Shenzhen and other cities. Can Hong Kong stop this trend of escapism, or even bring these people back?

Hong Kong has the space and opportunity to introduce stunning, comfortable and varied new housing options. Picture villas with spacious yards, towers with hanging gardens, and more apartments with sea views – a new, diversified housing program that attracts people to Hong Kong, to live, and to stay! Combining housing with leisure, work and shopping stimulates new marina developments, coastal developments, island developments, mixed-use developments, even housing 'bridges'. Finally Hong Kong's citizens can enjoy the beauty of their city while living in close proximity to its cultural venues, shops, beaches and natural landscapes. By upgrading and diversifying its stock, Hong Kong could grow to nearly ten million inhabitants by the year 2030!

Tower Revolution

Why not transform the current stock of housing towers to make existing apartments more liveable, more desirable?

With simple adaptations, Hong Kong can offer a new and spacious lifestyle. Why not add floor space to

each apartment; knock down walls to create larger units with more rooms?

Why not build balconies . . . add social areas . . . thicken towers . . . enlarge towers? A tower revolution!

Sea View Galore

Picture a chain of housing that meanders along the entire coastline of Hong Kong.

Serpentine waterfront complexes improve the dwelling / price ratio, address multiple sanitation

and health issues, and attract a variety of people. In addition, these open-structured building-scapes

facilitate airflow to the rest of the city.
From their spacious homes, residents enjoy

staggering sea views and open their windows to ocean-fresh air.

Invest in Infrastructure

Today, Hong Kong's public transport system is one of the most extensive and actively used in the world. But it needs improvement in order to reach world-class status. Its subways, busses, trams, and even ferries provide efficient alternatives to automobile transport, allowing highways to remain relatively jam free. Future growth in Hong Kong should preserve, and even enhance, this quality through further development of transportation systems: additional metro lines, better connections, and new roads – even in the heart of the city. It can improve current transportation system by increasing the use of ferries and water taxis, thereby enhancing the mobility of residents and tourists in the harbour districts and foreshore zones.

Adding bridges and links, integrating parking blocks with surrounding infrastructure, and introducing more parks and plazas could generate a more attractive and functional city.
These changes need to be complemented by a radical improvement of pedestrian networks to make the city's streets 'walkable' and attractive.
Now, Hong Kong's limited pedestrian zones are severed by infrastructure, parking structures and monstrous interiorized shopping malls with sad closed walls that dominate the streetscapes.
Hong Kong also needs to develop and extend its public transport system to include its many islands. With better connectivity, Hong Kong could transform itself into a thriving archipelago.

Hong Kong Bridged

Picture Hong Kong with a well-connected inter-regional ring road system.
A new highway provides access to the hinterland and other important focal points in the Pearl River Delta region, such as Guangzhou and Macau. It links

he municipalities along the Pearl Delta River, helps to strengthen regional diversity, and enhances each city's character and specialization. A new bridge connects Hong Kong with Macau, supporting the intercity exchange of cultural activity, goods and

services. Most of Hong Kong's 200 islands are isolated, difficult to reach. By connecting the coastal highway and the metro system to a web of new bridges that span the water, new developments sprout, spontaneously.

These bridges are programmed to project particular identities; there are housing bridges, office bridges, cultural bridges, as well as nautical bridges with marinas, harbours, fisheries and fish markets – all with breathtaking sea views.

They absorb existing buildings and inspire new functions: tired office space and interiorized faceless shopping malls become vibrant trade venues, tourist centres, recreational facilities, even luxury

apartments. Creating a web of city nodes on the water inspires citizens to work together to cultivate neighbourhoods that attract new residents, reinvigorating Hong Kong's public domain.

Urban Canyons

Why not cut into the mountains? Suddenly, the city opens up in new ways: canyon create shortcuts, connecting areas that were once

separated. These slices also function as air funnels, redirecting fresh air to different parts of the city and providing cool, clean zones in which to live, work and relax.

On top, forest bridges – eco-ducts – connect the paths on the hills. The edges of the ravines are hollowed out and filled with housing, universities

libraries and offices and enclosed with glass façades. A new world wonder appears . . . a sparkling twenty-first-century cave-village.

Invest in Nature

Hong Kong is teeming with nature; more than 80 per cent of its territory is green. But rather than investing in this asset, the city neglects it, allowing a careless pattern of new settlements to overtake its mountains and green areas.

But Hong Kong could limit urban development in its natural open spaces (such as wetlands and mountain areas) in order to preserve the landscape and to stabilize and enhance biodiversity. It could create pockets of beauty in the form of natural parks, right in the heart of the city.

Clean Air Boosters

During the summer, poor air quality is unavoidable in Hong Kong's high-rise neighbourhoods. But giant fans positioned in the bay boost the cooling process. Fuelled by wind-powered mills,

they blow artificial 'wind' through the streets, lowering the temperature of the blocks. Less energy is needed for air conditioning.
Street ventilation helps to improve clean air levels

and promote a healthier population, increasing the life expectancy of Hong Kong's citizens. The city becomes a fresh and healthy environment.

Central Mountain Park

Let's declare Hong Kong a national park! Let's add wildlife and make an eco zoo; let's create a series of ecological paths, drives, and hikes as investments in natural diversity.

By introducing nature centres, museums, lodges, spas and hotels, we can enhance the image, the quality and the attractiveness of Hong Kong.

A large mountainous nature reserve already exists in the middle of Hong Kong, only steps away from thousands of offices. Why not create a system of pedestrian bridges that opens up this green area, simplifying access.

At last, the people of Hong Kong can enjoy the ecological benefits of its inner city mountains. Welcome to Hong Kong Eco-Park.

Super Hong Kong

With the Why Factory's World-Class City Framework at the foundation of urban and architectural development, which fosters and enhances densification, diversification and connectivity, a new and powerful vision of our future cities – in this case Hong Kong – can unfold. Driven by density, diversity and connectivity, cities can generate an optimal spatial and programmatic mix.

To cultivate this vision, the stakeholders, inhabitants and thinkers who work on city development need to integrate a compelling architecture that supports a free, safe, and prosperous city.

Instead of only consuming, our cities can develop to their full potential as sustainable producers of culture, clean energy, healthy food, comfortable housing and knowledge, to promote sophisticated, responsible, and comfortable citizens.

Agenda

'World-class organizations identify and develop a clear, concise and shared meaning of values/beliefs, priorities, and direction so that everyone understands and can contribute effectively. Once defined and properly integrated, values positively impact every aspect of your organization.' [44]

World-Class Benchmarking

The World-Class City Framework (WCCF) is not a recipe, but an attempt to standardize and bring together important factors that actually make cities world-class. A system of standardization for world-class cities is difficult to conceive since every city refers to its own set of data that originates from its particular geographical, political and socio-economic history. Nonetheless, the WCCF is a starting point – a place-making guideline – for the creation of world-class conditions. It serves as a critical reminder to consider the impact of our actions on the future growth of cities.

As populations grow and resources dwindle, developing and managing world-class cities effectively is critical. The task of the WCCF is to close the gap between the exhaustion of our resources and the need to introduce world-class living standards that fit the needs and desires of the city's users.

To bring the World-Class City Framework forward, this book aims to develop a comprehensive standardization system for world-class city indicators. This system is the next step toward monitoring performance of cities and facilitating comparison and verification across the globe. Such standardization could enable cities, developers and stakeholders to observe and capture trends over time, to establish benchmarks, share best practices, and evaluate developments.

As cities all over the world develop at an increasing pace, they try to brand themselves as high quality living and working places. The aim of the WCCF is to anchor change and guide city branding with a collection of indicators that are sufficiently broad to capture economic, environmental and socio-spatial aspects of world-class urban life. In order to ensure consistent quality of development, this collection of indicators measuring world-class performance need to be approved by the International Organization for Standardization (ISO).

With the WCCF, cities can become part of a more interconnected and responsible world and compete for new types of investments that focus on high density, international as well local events, a diverse culture, social and spatial connectedness.

The WCCF can help managers, politicians, decision-makers and residents make sustainable choices in the development of their cities. It puts quality of life back on the agenda and links it to an architecture that brings joy, pride and excitement to the city's inhabitants and visitors.

Notes & Credits

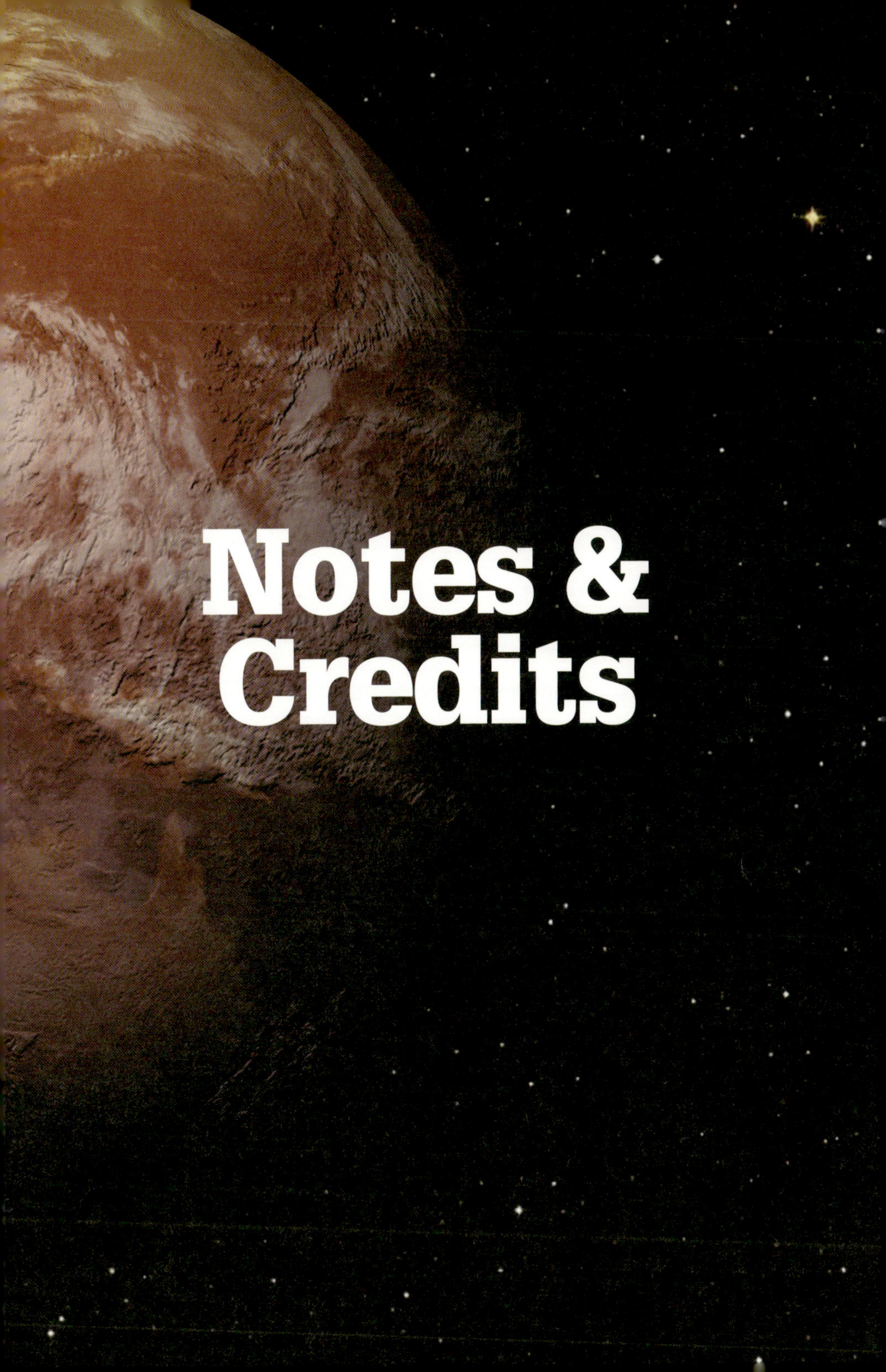

Notes

[1] 'Looking at cities at eye level', Interview with Jan Gehl by Eva Isager, International news magazine from cowi, Online Available HTTP: http://www.cowi.com/menu/NewsandMedia/News/Buildings/Documents/Interview_with_Jan_Gehl.pdf (accessed 25 January 2011).

[2] McDonald's, for example, has set up a document of 'Standards of Business Conduct' which serves as a guide to 'making good decisions and conducting business ethically.' In addition, McDonald's runs a world-class training-program that each employee is obliged to follow. Wherever on the planet McDonald's goes, it becomes an integral part of the community it operates in and contributes towards the development of the locality. For example, McDonald's has introduced the concept of so-called 'Litter Patrol'. This means that McDonald's employees survey the immediate vicinity of the restaurant every day, picking up garbage left behind not only by customers from McDonald's restaurants but also by other visitors to the area. The result is a cleaner neighbourhood. This happens in London, England as well as in the neighbourhoods of Mumbai, India or anywhere else McDonald's operates. McDonald's, 'Our World'. Online. Available HTTP: http://www.mcdonalds.co.uk/ourworld/environment/litter.shtml (accessed 25 January 2011).

[3] 'Being, belonging and becoming' are the three major life domains identified by the Quality of Life Research Unit in: 'QOL Concepts – The Quality of Life Model', University of Toronto, Centre for Health Promotion. Online. Available HTTP: http://www.utoronto.ca/qol/concepts.htm (accessed 25 January 2011).

[4] 'Sassen's Circuits Connecting to a World Class Future', Bill Hangley Jr., Online Available HTTP: http://economyleague.org/files/Insight_Volume3_Final.pdf (accessed 25 January 2011).

[5] 'Quality of Living worldwide city rankings 2010', (26 May 2010) *Mercer*. Online press release. Available HTTP: http://www.mercer.com/press-releases/quality-of-living-report-2010#City_Ranking_Tables (accessed 25 January 2011).

[6] 'Mercer 2010 Quality of Living survey highlights – Global', (26 May 2010), *Mercer*. Online. Available HTTP: http://www.mercer.nl/articles/quality-of-living-survey-report-2010. (accessed 25 January 2011).

[7] 'Global Cities Index 2010', *Foreign Policy Magazine*. Online. Available HTTP: http://www.foreignpolicy.com/articles/2010/08/11/the_global_cities_index_2010 (accessed 25 January 2011).

[8] '2010 Global Cities Index', *A.T. Kearney*. Online. Available HTTP: http://www.atkearney.com/index.php/Publications/global-cities-index.html (accessed 25 January 2011).

[9] 'Global Cities Index 2010', op. cit. (note 7).

Foreign Policy Magazine's Top 10 Cities in 2010:
01 New York City, USA
02 London, England
03 Tokyo, Japan
04 Paris, France
05 Hong Kong SAR, China
06 Chicago, USA
07 Los Angeles, USA
08 Singapore
09 Sydney, Australia
10 Seoul, South Korea

[10] Z/yen Group, 'Global Financial Centres Index 8' (September 2010). Online PDF. Available HTTP: http://www.zyen.com/GFCI/GFCI%208.pdf (accessed 25 January 2011).

Z/Yen Group's Top 10 Global Financial Cities in 2010,:
01 London, England
02 New York, USA
03 Hong Kong SAR, China
04 Singapore
05 Tokyo, Japan
06 Shanghai, China
07 Chicago, USA
08 Zurich, Switzerland
09 Geneva, Switzerland
10 Sydney, Australia

[11] 'It's Vancouver Again', (11 February 2010), *Gulliver*. Blog. *The Economist*. Online. Available HTTP: http://www.economist.com/blogs/gulliver/2010/02/liveability_rankings (accessed 25 January 2011).

[12] ibid.

[13] ibid.

Economist Intelligence Unit's 'Quality-of-life Index' Top 10 Most Liveable Cities in 2010:
01 Vancouver, Canada
02 Vienna, Austria
03 Melbourne, Australia
04 Toronto, Canada
05 Calgary, Canada
06 Helsinki, Finland
07 Sydney, Australia
08 Perth, Australia
08 Adelaide, Australia
10 Auckland, New Zealand

[14] Lauren Sherman, 'World's Most Stylish Cities', (30 June 2009), *Forbes.com*. Online. Available HTTP: http://www.forbes.com/2009/06/30/cities-stylish-ten-lifestyle-style-real-estate-fashion.html (accessed 25 January 2011).

Forbes's Top 10 Most Stylish Cities in 2009:
01 Paris, France
02 Milan, Italy
03 New York, USA
04 London, England
05 Rome, Italy

06 Los Angeles, USA
07 Tokyo, Japan
08 Madrid, Spain
09 San Francisco, USA
10 Barcelona, Spain

[15] Jamie Song, '25 Most Liveable Cities', (16 June 2010), *PSFK.com*. Online. Available HTTP: http://www.psfk.com/2010/06/top-25-most-liveable-cities-2010.html (accessed 25 January 2011).

Monocle's Top Ten Most Liveable Cities in 2010:
01 Munich, Germany
02 Copenhagen, Denmark
03 Zurich, Switzerland
04 Tokyo, Japan
05 Helsinki, Finland
06 Stockholm, Sweden
07 Paris, France
08 Vienna, Austria
09 Melbourne, Australia
10 Madrid, Spain

[16] Lonely Planet, *The Cities Book: A Journey through the Best Cities in the World*, Lonely Planet Publications Pty Ltd (Melbourne, March 2006).

[17] Dominic Armato, ,et. al., (16 June 2010), 'Top 29: Best Cities to Live In', (16 June 2010), *Askmen.com*. Online. Available HTTP: http://uk.askmen.com/specials/2009_top_29/chicago.html (accessed 25 January 2011).

Ask-Men.com's Top 10 World's Hottest Cities to Live In in 2009:
01 Chicago, USA
02 Barcelona, Spain
03 San Francisco, USA
04 London, England
05 Sydney, Australia
06 New York, USA
07 Berlin, Germany
08 Hong Kong SAR, China
09 Copenhagen, Denmark
10 Paris, France

[18] Robert F. Kennedy Address, University of Kansas, Lawrence, Kansas, 18 March 1968

[19] Over the years, the often-cited Gross Domestic Product (GDP) has emerged as a barometer for well-being, on a national level. When a country's GDP is growing rapidly, it is said to be 'doing well'. When it is declining, it is 'doing poorly'. But the GDP is not a sufficient indicator – on a national or urban level – of quality of life. It was not designed to reflect the well-being of people; it is a simple representation of national income and consumption. Its objective is, by definition, to measure the value of all goods and services produced in a country in a given year. As a measurement of consumption, the GDP is based on a paradigm that says, 'more is better'. Spending on war, natural and human-made disasters, fossil fuel-based energy production, security and police, all cause the GDP to rise. It is thus a calculative tool that describes any kind of expenditure as a positive contribution to commerce. These are hardly signs that city-dwellers are better off, or that considerations have been made for activities that heat up our planet, pollute our air and waterways, or destroy farmlands, wetlands and forests. The very notion of economic, social and environmental sustainability does not enter the equation. The GDP disregards many things that really matter to the quality of life and well-being of the city dweller.

[20] Urban Dictionary, Definition of 'World Class City', Online. Available HTTP: http://www.urbandictionary.com/define.php?term=world%20class%20city

[21] Kevin Lynch, 'The Form of Cities', *Scientific America*, Vol. 190, No. 4, (April 1954), 54-63, Online. Available HTTP: *http://www.isc.meiji.ac.jp/~cova/column/the_forms_of_cities.pdf*

[22] Winy Maas, 'Be More!', *AA#378 Magazine*, 110.

[23] The term *diversity* includes the activity of diverting and originates from the Latin word *divertere* meaning 'to turn aside'. Divertere implicates movement and is thus relating strongly to connectivity.

[24] UN HABITAT, *Migrants and Multicultural Cities: Problem or Possibility? UN-HABITAT Report celebrates multiculturalism*,Online. Available HTTP: http://www.unhabitat.org/documents/media_centre/sowc/Featuremigrants.pdf

[25] ibid.

[26] ibid.

[27] According to the *Merriam-Webster Dictionary*, the word *connection* originates from the Latin word *connectere*; *con* meaning 'together' and *nectere* meaning 'bind'. Connecting thus is rooted in community (belonging), which suggests a link to communication.

[28] Richard Florida, *The Rise Of The Creative Class: And How It's Transforming Work, Leisure, Community And Everyday Life* (New York: Basic Books, 2002), ##

[29] According to the Quality of Life Research Unit of the University of Toronto, 'being, belonging and becoming' identify the three major life domains of the citizen:
'The **Being** domain includes the basic aspects of 'who one is' and has three sub-domains. Physical Being includes aspects of physical health, personal hygiene, nutrition, exercise, grooming, clothing, and physical appearance. Psychological Being includes the person's psychological health and adjustment, cognitions, feelings, and evaluations concerning the self, and self-control. Spiritual Being reflects personal values, personal standards of conduct, and spiritual beliefs which may or may not be associated with organized religions.
'**Belonging** includes the person's fit with his/her environments and also

has three sub-domains. Physical Belonging is defined as the connections the person has with his/her physical environments such as home, workplace, neighborhood, school and community. Social Belonging includes links with social environments and includes the sense of acceptance by intimate others, family, friends, co-workers, and neighborhood and community. Community Belonging represents access to resources normally available to community members, such as adequate income, health and social services, employment, educational and recreational programs, and community activities. '**Becoming** refers to the purposeful activities carried out to achieve personal goals, hopes, and wishes. Practical Becoming describes day-to-day actions such as domestic activities, paid work, school or volunteer activities, and seeing to health or social needs. Leisure Becoming includes activities that promote relaxation and stress reduction. These include card games, neighborhood walks, and family visits, or longer duration activities such as vacations or holidays. Growth Becoming activities promote the improvement or maintenance of knowledge and skills.'

[30] In the early seventieth century, the city of Mannheim, Germany embodied these values. Founded in 1605 by Elector Friedrich IV as a centre of commerce and trade Mannheim set no limits on immigration. At a time that most other European cities were segregating their minority populations, this openness brought on a revolutionary multicultural integration. Its government supported the timeless ideals of personal freedom, tax incentives and other amenities. As a result, Mannheim soon became a European centre of multicultural coexistence. Many different nations, with their own traditions and languages, contributed to a politics of coexistence and tolerance; gradually their ideas became embedded in the city's government. The legislative body of Mannheim was composed of representatives the different nations that inhabited Mannheim to ensure a multinational actualization of the city and encourage the participation of all inhabitants, regardless their ethnic backgrounds.
Although Mannheim had been strongly afflicted by wars and the Black Death in 1666, it continued to grow; its urban area was built up rapidly in a Manhattan-like grid; large companies settled and trade increased. As part of the regeneration plan, Elector Karl Ludwig, who came to Mannheim in 1649 to continue the work of his grandfather, commissioned Jacob van Deyl – a Dutch engineer living in Mannheim – to draw up a blueprint for a future layout of the city. Van Deyl's plan reflected Mannheim's values of religious tolerance and political, economic and cultural equality. It excluded territorial borders related to the ethnic or religious background of its population. Instead, it proposed a variegated society that welcomed newcomers and encouraged the growth of its many cultural groups. Van Deyl's plan incorporated opportunities for all inhabitants to participate in the creation of their city and encouraged its inhabitants to integrate and mix. He implemented the idea to name the streets of Mannheim after their inhabitants. Consequently, city planning and its architecture came to express the desires and interests of the city's diverse population: French, Dutch, German and Walloon bakeries and butcheries appeared; Jewish inhabitants built synagogues and Mikwas (a Mikwa is a Jewish bath used for physical and spiritual cleanliness); Catholics and Protestants built their churches to establish their own congregation. As Mannheim flourished, it again became the European centre of multicultural coexistence – a world-class city of its time. Unfortunately, in 1689, only eight decades after it was founded, this 'modern city' was fully destroyed during the Palatine war of succession. (http://www.zeit.de/2002/06/Das_Mannheimer_Experiment)

[31] TUNG Chee Hwa, 'Chief Executive's Policy Address 1999', GovHk, Online. Available HTTP: http://www.policyaddress.gov.hk/pa99/english/part4-1.htm

[32] 'Mercer 2010 Quality of Living survey highlights – Global', (26 May 2010), *Mercer*. Online. Available HTTP: http://www.mercer.nl/articles/quality-of-living-survey-report-2010; Economist Intelligence Unit, 'The Economist Intelligence Unit's quality-of-life index', *The Economist*. Online PDF. Available HTTP: http://www.economist.com/media/pdf/quality_of_life.pdf; 'Global Cities Index Methodology', (18 August 2010), *Foreign Policy Magazine*. Online. Available HTTP: http://www.foreignpolicy.com/articles/2010/08/18/global_cities_index_methodology (all accessed 25 January 2011).

[33] In the year 2000, Nanjing Road was renovated as a shopping street as part of the government's redevelopment plan. It has become one of the world's longest shopping streets with a length of six km, attracting over one million visitors daily.

[34] Over the past 15 years Singapore has invested in an impressive streetscape in many parts of the city such as Orchard Road, Chinatown, Malay Quarter, Little India and the Waterfront areas along Singapore River. Promenade railing, paving, greenery, lighting and public furniture enhance the atmospheres of these places.

[35] GovHK, 'Hong Kong: The Facts – Trade and Industry', (January 2011). Online PDF. Available HTTP: http://www.gov.hk/en/about/abouthk/factsheets/docs/trade&industry.pdf (accessed 25 January 2011).

[36] WWF-Hong Kong, 'Hong Kong Ecological Footprint Report 2010 – Paths to a sustainable Future' (January 2011). Online PDF. Available HTTP: http://assets.panda.org/downloads/wwf_a4_report_2010_web.pdf (accessed 25 January 2011).

[37] 'Hong Kong Cultural Sovereignty: Whose Tamar is it?', Speech delivered by Ying-Tai Lung at Hong Kong University on June 2, 2006. Online PDF. Available HTTP: http://www.harbourdistrict.com.hk/enews/20060613/20060607_1.pdf (accessed 25 January 2011).

[38] 'Hong Kong's biggest-ever property boom', (27 April 2010), *Global Property Guide*. Online. Available HTTP: http://www.globalpropertyguide.com/Asia/Hong-Kong/Rental-Yields (accessed 25 January 2011).

[39] GovHK, 'Hong Kong: The Facts – Population Factsheet', (January 2011). Online PDF. Available HTTP: http://www.gov.hk/en/about/abouthk/factsheets/docs/population.pdf (accessed 25 January 2011).

[40] GovHK, Heritage Museum, 'Memories of Home – 50 Years of Public Housing in Hong Kong'. Online PDF. Available HTTP: http://www.heritagemuseum.gov.hk/downloads/materials/Public_Housing-E.pdf (accessed 25 January 2011).

[41] GovHk, 'The Natural Environment, Plants & Animals in Hong Kong', (September 2010). Online. Available HTTP: http://www.gov.hk/en/residents/environment/conservation/naturalenvplantsanimals.htm (accessed 25 January 2011).

[42] As the coastline of Hong Kong is a key part of its social, cultural and economic heritage, it needs special management and development, addressing and activating local residents as well as tourists.

[43] Tony M. W. Kwok, 'Hong Kong's Competitive Advantage: A clean Society', Online. Available HTTP: http://www.kwok-manwai.com/articles/clean_society.html (accessed 25 January 2011).

[44] World Class Benchmarking, 'World Class Excellence Model', Online. Available HTTP: http://www.worldclassbenchmarking.com/home_section/excellence_model.html

Sources

Fig. 04
Global Financial Centers Index
Source: z/yen, 2010

Fig. 05
Global Cities Index
Source: FP magazine, The A.T. Kearney Global Cities Index, 2010

Fig. 06
Quality of Living Index
Source: mercer, 2010

Fig. 07
Cost of Living Index
Source: Economist, 2010

Fig. 08
Education Index
Source: Human Development Reports, 2010

Fig. 09
Amount of buildings >90m
Source: Skyscaper Cities Rankinglist, 2011

Fig. 10
Number of Operas
Source: The Why Factory Research, 2010

Fig. 11
Number of Museums
Source: The Why Factory Research, 2010

Fig. 12
Number of theaters
Source: The Why Factory Research, 2010

Fig. 13
Number of Cinemas
Source: The Why Factory Research, 2010

Fig. 14
Largest Seaports in the World
Source: Geohive.com, (various data), 2011

Fig. 15
Largest Container Ports in the World
Source: Geohive.com, (various data), 2011

Fig. 16
World's Stock Exchanges
Source: DMC, Wikipedia, 2010

Fig. 17
Economic Freedom Index
Source: Heritage Foundation, 2010

Fig. 18
Energy Imports
Source: Worldbank, 2010

Fig. 19
Ecological Footprint
Source: WWF, Living Planet Report, 2010

Fig. 20
Dwelling Space
Source: The Why Factory Research, 2010

Fig. 21
Public Transport
Source: CityMayors.com, 2010

Fig. 22
Urban Rail per City Nation Index
Source: CityMayors.com, 2010

Fig. 23
Green Space
Source: The Why Factory Research, 2010

Fig. 24
Coastline Index
Source: The Why Factory Research, 2010

Bibliography

Le Bas, T., 'Hong Kong, Macau & Guangzhou', *Insight City Guide* (Singapore: Apa Publications GmbH & Co, 2005)

Birkinshaw, M. and V. Harris, 'The Right to the "World Class City"?', *The Urban Reinventors Online Journal* (2009) no. 3. Available online at http://urbanreinventors.net/3/birkinshaw/birkinshaw-urbanreinventors.pdf (accessed 5 September 2011)

Butler, J., S.O. Hastings, B. Pryor, and C. P. Short, 'The Effects of a Crowded Deliberation Environment on Mock Jurors' Attitudes and Decision-Making', *Communication Law Review*, vol. 6 (2006) no. 2, 58–69. Available online at http://www.carltonfields.com/files/Publication/761e10a8-8e1e-4cd2-9a8e-101f4b3468ce/Presentation/PublicationAttachment/173fcbff-4edf-48ce-9b00-10836843d83f/The%20Effects%20of%20a%20Crowded%20Deliberation%20Environment%20on%20Mock%20Jurors'%20Attitudes%20and%20Decision.pdf (accessed 5 September 2011)

Construction Department, Guangdong Province, Development Bureau Hong Kong SAR, Secretariat for Transport and Public Works, Macau SAR, 'Planning study on he co-ordinated development of the Greater Pearl River Delta townships – Consolidated Final Report', *Building Coordinated and Sustainable World-class City-regions* (2009). Available online at http://www.dssopt.gov.mo/uploads/wizdownload/201012/116_rmjgg.pdf (accessed 5 September 2011)

Fahy, F., 'Deriving Quality of Life Indicators in Urban Areas, A Practitioner's Guide', *Galway 21: Implementing the Principles and Practices of Sustainable Development in Galway City Council* (Department of Geography, National University of Ireland, Galway and Environmental Protection Agency, 2008). Available online at http://www.epa.ie/downloads/pubs/research/econ/galway21_fahy_guide.pdf (accessed 5 September 2011)

Goldfinger, S., S. Niazi, M. Stechbart, et al, 'Hong Kong Ecological Footprint Report 2008' (Global Footprint Network, WWF Hong Kong, 2008). Available online at http://www.footprintnetwork.org/images/uploads/Ecological_Footprint_HongKong.pdf (accessed 5 September 2011)

Hong Kong Sustainable Development Forum, 'Response', *Making Choices for our Future – First Strategy, Invitation and Response Consultation Paper* (2004). Available online at http://hksdf.org.hk/downloads/HKSDF_consultation_FINAL.pdf (accessed 5 September 2011)

Jensen, O. B., 'Discourse Analysis & Socio-Spatial Transformation Processes: A Theoretical Framework For Analysing Spatial Planning', *Electronic Working Paper No 28* (Global Urban Research Unit, School Of Architecture, Planning & Landscape, University Of Newcastle Upon Tyne. Previously published as: O. B. Jensen, Working Paper No. 61, Department of Development and Planning, Aalborg University, August 1997). Available online at http://www.ncl.ac.uk/guru/assets/documents/ewp28.pdf (accessed 5 September 2011)

Landhäußer, S. and H. Ziegler, 'Social Work and the Quality of Life Politics – A Critical Assessment', Social Work & Society, vol. 3 (2005) no. 1, 30–58. Available Online at http://www.socwork.net/2005/1/articles/472/LandhaeusserZiegler2005.pdf (accessed 5 September 2011)

Leman, E., 'Can the Pearl River Delta Region Still Compete?', *The China Business Review*, (2003) May–June, 6–17. Available online at http://www.chreod.com/publications/20052222_4000727may03_CBR%20FINAL_PRD.pdf (accessed 5 September 2011)

Lin, Keith P.Y., 'Global City Review: Hong Kong as a Global City', *Working Paper Series* (London School of Economics & Political Science, 2008). Available online at http://ssrn.com/abstract=1101011 (accessed 5 September 2011)

Lung, Y. T., 'Hong Kong Cultural Sovereignty: Whose Tamar is it?', speech delivered at Hong Kong University on 2 June 2006. Available online at http://www.harbourdistrict.com.hk/enews/20060613/20060607_1.pdf (accessed 5 September 2011)

Mahtab-Uz-Zaman, Q. M., 'Hong Kong: A Review Of Density, Urban Form And Sustainable Development' (Hong Kong: Department of Architecture, University of Hong Kong, 2006). Available online at http://www.neduet.edu.pk/Arch_2Jne/Arch11/JRAP-2003/JRAP%203/Hong%20Kong%20Density.pdf (accessed 5 September 2011)

Ou-fan Lee, L., 'City between Worlds – My Hong Kong' (The Belknap Press of Harvard University Press, 2008)

Peck, J. and H. Shah, 'Well-being and the Environment', *The Power of Well-being 4* (London: WWF, New Economics Foundation, 2005). Available online at http://www.i-r-e.org/docs/a005_well-being-and-the-environment.pdf (accessed 5 September 2011)

Ping Yan, F., 'Public Housing in Hong Kong – Past, Present and Future', (Executive Committee Chartered Institute of Housing, Asian Pacific Branch, South Asian Health Foundation, City University of Hong Kong, 2006). Available online at http://www.cih.org.hk/event_speaker_dnload/events2006100801/Public%20Housing%20in%20Hong%20Kong-%20Presentation%2024-9-06(insert%20photo).pdf (accessed 5 September 2011)

Regardh, P., 'Networked Society City Index – Learning from the Best', *Bench marking Creative Cities* (Ericson, EBR #2, 2011). Available online at http://www.ericsson.com/res/thecompany/docs/publications/business-review/2011/issue1/networked-society.pdf (accessed 5 September 2011)

Strategic Planning Division of the City of Winnipeg and the Measurement and Indicators Program of the International Institute for Sustainable Development (IISD), *City of Winnipeg Quality of Life Indicators* (1999). Available online at: http://www.iisd.org/pdf/wpg.qoli.pdf (accessed 5 September 2011)

Sun, Y., 'Development Of Neighbourhood Quality Of Life Indicators' (Community-University Institute for Social Research, University of Saskatchewan, 2005). Available online at http://www.usask.ca/cuisr/docs/pub_doc/quality/sun.pdf (accessed 5 September 2011)

UN-HABITAT, 'Migrants and Multicultural Cities: Problem or Possibility?', *United Nations Human Settlements Programme* (2004). Available online at http://www.unhabitat.org/documents/media_centre/sowc/Featuremigrants.pdf (accessed 5 September 2011)

Wu, C. T., 'China's Special Economic Zones: Five Years After – An Introduction', *Asian Journal Of Public Administration* (2004), 127–143. Available online at sunzi.lib.hku.hk/hkjo/view/50/5000240.pdf (accessed on 5 September, 2011)

Institutions

The Why think tank an research run by Delft University Technology in colla MVRDV. It aims argumentation b architecture an the production visualizations. and fiction, The W analyses, theorize im , and constructs new visi ns future cities.

Julianalaan 132-134/ 2628 BL Delft/ The Netherlands
www.thewhyfactory.com

The Berlage Institute is a post-academic laboratory for design-based research in architecture, urbanism, and other issues related to the built environment. Its postgraduate program and PhD program are open to applications from graduated and experienced architects, urban planners, landscape architects, and other researchers. Complementary to these programs, the Institute also broadens its activities to the professional sector; initiates a series of publications, for which it solicits internal and external collaborators; and organizes a public program of lectures, debates, and symposia.

Berlage Institute / Botersloot 23 / 3011HE Rotterdam / The Netherlands
www.berlage-institute.nl

The Chinese University of Hong Kong (CUHK) with its School of Architecture has developed over a course of 20 years a research and teaching ethos that valued excellence, innovation, and contribution to the community. The mission of the School is to advance knowledge and prepare students for contemporary challenges. Research

ofessional expertise in bui vironment design in its com d multi-dimensional scope; chitectural computation, digital fabrication, material and structural research, and social and cultural studies all serve to alignment the fundamental notion of design, being at the centre of all activities related to the School.

Our teaching pedagogy is consistently reviewed and enhanced. Students explore design solutions through rigorous research on international practices and pertinent issues facing the built environment in the region involving studio collaboration with leading schools of architecture around the world. We have a long track record in serving and involving the community. Public engagement, participation and community design exercises were frequently held for the betterment of urban and design environment in Hong Kong. Construction projects in remote villages and earthquake affected areas in China help to improve living environment for local inhabitants. The School of Architecture at the Chinese University of Hong Kong stands at the confluence of innovation and practice in built environment design of the present and the future, in China and the world. The School strives to broaden its research and teaching concerns to build a conducive and sustainable future for the community and beyond.

The Chinese University of Hong Kong/ Room 514, Wong Foo Yuan Building/ Shatin, New Territories/ Hong Kong SAR/ China
http://www.arch.cuhk.edu.hk/index.html

as well as of Urban Planning and mental Management. The activity of the Faculty is training both professionals and researchers. Training activities include undergraduate, Master's and Ph.D programs in the fields of architecture design, urban design and planning, architecture history and conservation, building science, construction project management, real estate, etc.
The Department encourages interdisciplinary studies, exchange programs for students and staff in order to develop international co-operations for research and training with other research institutes, organizations and universities. It also supports organizations of exhibitions, symposiums and other events in cooperation with national and international bodies.

Department of Architecture/ 3/F Knowles Building/ The University of Hong Kong/ Pokfulam Road/ Hong Kong SAR/ China
http://fac.arch.hku.hk

The International Forum on Urbanism (IFoU) is a network of universities, research institutes and knowledge centers with the task to strengthen the international collaboration in the field of Urbanism. Governmental and professional institutions that are related to the planning and design of the built environment, can be associated members.

Julianalaan 132-134/ 2628 BL Delft/ The Netherlands
http://www.ifou.org

Credits

This book is based on the first-year postgraduate studio 'Hong Kong Fantasies', held in the fall of 2008 at the Berlage Institute, Rotterdam; on the master class of the same title held at the Chinese University of Hong Kong in October 2008; and on the animated movie 'Hong Kong Power' first shown at the Business of Design Week 2008 in Hong Kong.

The master class has been organized by the International Forum on Urbanism (IFoU).

First-year postgraduate studio 'Hong Kong Fantasies', the Berlage Institute, fall 2008
Tutors: Winy Maas with Tihamér Salij and Ulf Hackauf
Students: Zetao Chen, Pedram Dibazar, Marco Galasso, Dong Woo Kang, Eunjin Kang, Andreas Karavanas, Young Il Kim, Nara Lee, Chen-Jung Liu, Luca Picardi, Nuria Pujol Caire, Jad Semaan, Timur Shabaev, Janki Shah, Xiaodi Yang

Master Class, 'Hong Kong Fantasies', the Chinese University of Hong Kong, October 2008:
Participating Universities: Delft University of Technology, The Why Factory (TU Delft), Urban Body (TU Delft), IFoU Summer School, Berlage Institute, Chinese University of Hong Kong (CUHK), Hong Kong University (HKU), Beijing University of Technology (TU Beijing)

Executive Board: Prof. Jürgen Rosemann (Chairman, International Forum on Urbanism, IFoU), Prof. Tsou Jin-yeu (Director, Center for Housing Innovations, Chinese University of Hong Kong), Stephen S.Y. Lau (Associate Professor, Faculty of Architecture, Hong Kong University), Prof. Lim Wan-fung, Bernard (Director of the Community Participation Unit CUHK), Prof. Winy Maas (The Why Factory/TU Delft/ Berlage Institute/MVRDV), Rob Docter (Director, Berlage Institute), Wang Chiu-Yuan Vivienne (Executive director, International Forum on Urbanism IFoU)

Overall Organization: Wang Chiu-Yuan (International Forum on Urbanism)
Financial Coordination: Agnes Wijers (TU Delft)
Organization Master Class: Françoise Vos (Berlage Institute) with Andy Wong (CUHK)
Master Teacher: Prof. Winy Maas (The Why Factory, TU Delft)
Content & Program Coordination: Tihamér Salij (The Why Factory, TU Delft)
Coordinating Tutors: Tihamér Salij (The Why Factory, TU Delft) with Hendrik Tieben (Chinese University of Hong Kong)
Tutors: Ulf Hackauf (The Why Factory, TU Delft), Maurice Harteveld (Dep. Urbanism, TU Delft), Alexander Vollebregt (Urban Body, TU Delft), He Jie (Center for Housing Innovations, CUHK), Yu Han (Center for Housing Innovations, CUHK), Wong, Andy (Community Participation Unit CUHK), Hui Xiaoxi (School of Architecture, TU Beijing), Salie Wang (Architecture & Urban Design Studio on Sustainability, HKU), Hoyin Lee (Architecture & Urban Design Studio on Sustainability, HKU)

Students:
Delft University of Technology: Mick van Gemert, Tanya Martinez Gonzales, Alessandro Bua, Angelle Elshot, Anthony Fuchs, Jasper Moelker, Nicola Knop, Friso Gouwetor, Charlotte Heesbeen, Chunyan Song, Maarten den Teuling, Alejandro Elias Garcia Marta

Berlage Institute: Zetao Chen, Pedram Dibazar, Marco Galasso, Dong Woo Kang, Eunjin Kang, Andreas Karavanas, Young Il Kim, Nara Lee, Chen-Jung Liu, Luca Picardi, Nuria Pujol Caire, Jad Semaan, Timur Shabaev, Janki Shah, Xiaodi Yang

Chinese University of Hong Kong: LAM Kwai Pui Patrick, LU Kam Wing Jim, NGAN Yuk Kei Penny, POON Ching Pong Adrian, YIU Kam Po Vince, ZHAN Xu Zhen Jasmine, IEM Stephanie, CHAMPALUE Edouard [illegible] ...an [illegible] Ca[illegible] TAO Yuen [illegible], WONG Wai Hou Za[illegible]Y Ka Fai Ivan, LAM Wa[illegible]ard, NG Kam Shing Oscar

Hong Kong University: CHAN Hon Lam, CHIU Wai Kwan, FUNG Yuen Man Azalea, HO Eunice Hoi Ling, IP Kenneth Tze Chung, MA Yao, NG Pui Yee, POON Chi Chung, TSANG Germain Ming Cheung, TSANG Pui Ki, WAN Kam Ping, YAN Shing Fung

Beijing University of Technology: LV Chao, SONG Xiaoyu, HUANG Jing, CHEN Lili, LIU Huajing

Results of the master class 'Hong Kong Fantasies' were presented as the animated movie Hong Kong Power at the Business of Design Week 2008 in Hong Kong.
Hong Kong Power was conceptualized and edited by The Why Factory (Winy Maas, Tihamér Salij and Ulf Hackauf) and animated by Wieland & Gouwens, Rotterdam.

Credits

This book was conceived, produced and edited by The Why Factory,
The Why Factory, Delft: Winy Maas with Tihamér Salij and Bas Kalmeyer

Authors:
Why Fantasize?, Investment Strategies for Hong Kong:
Winy Maas and Tihamér Salij
The Degradation of World-Class, Greatness is Subjective, Setting Higher Standards, How World-Class is Hong Kong?, Agenda:
Tihamér Salij

Associate editor: Jennifer Sigler
Images: Marino Wieland and Eline Gouwens, Wieland and Gouwens, Rotterdam
Graphic Design: BENG, Bas de Wolff
Design of The Why Factory logo: Thonik in collaboration with BENG
Lithography and Printing: Die Keure, Bruges, Belgium
Paper: Arctic Volume, 120 grs
Production: Marcel Witvoet, NAi Publishers, Rotterdam
Publisher: Eelco van Welie, NAi Publishers, Rotterdam

Hong Kong Fantasies is the fifth book in the Why Factory's 'Future Cities Series'. It follows *The Why Factor(y)* (2009), *Visionary Cities* (2009), *Green Dream* (2010), and *The Vertical Village* (2011).

This publication, the Master Class Hong Kong Fantasies and the movie Hong Kong Power have been financially supported by the Dutch government in the framework of the 'Open Minds' program.

NAi Publishers is an internationally orientated publisher specialized in developing, producing and distributing books on architecture, visual arts and related disciplines.
www.naipublishers.nl

Available in North, South and Central America through Artbook/D.A.P., 155 Sixth Avenue, 2nd Floor, New York, NY 10013-1507, tel +1 212 627 1999, fax +1 212 627 9484, dap@dapinc.com

Available in the United Kingdom and Ireland through Art Data, 12 Bell
Industrial Estate, 50 Cunnington Street, London W4 5HB, tel +44 208 747 1061, fax +44 208 742 2319, orders@artdata.co.uk

Printed and bound in Belgium
ISBN 978-90-5662-764-5